The
iPod™
Companion

Tony Bove

The iPod™ Companion

The iPod™ Companion

Senior Vice President, Retail Strategic Market Group: Andy Shafran

Publisher: Stacy L. Hiquet

Credits: Senior Marketing Manager, Sarah O'Donnell; Marketing Manager, Heather Hurley; Manager of Editorial Services, Heather Talbot; Senior Acquisitions Editor, Kevin Harreld; Associate Marketing Manager, Kristin Eisenzopf; Retail Market Coordinator, Sarah Dubois; Production Editor, Dan Foster, Scribe Tribe; Copy Editor, Dan Foster; Technical Editor, Mark Abdelnour; Proofreader, Kezia Endsley; Cover Designer, Mike Tanamachi; Interior Design and Layout, Danielle Foster, Scribe Tribe; Indexer, Sharon Shock.

Library of Congress Catalog Number: 2003108323

ISBN: 1-59200-113-0

5 4 3 2 1

Educational facilities, companies, and organizations interested in multiple copies or licensing of this book should contact the publisher for quantity discount information. Training manuals, CD-ROMs, and portions of this book are also available individually or can be tailored for specific needs.

MUSKA LIPMAN Publishing

Muska & Lipman Publishing,
a Division of Course Technology
25 Thomson Place
Boston, MA 02210
www.muskalipman.com
publisher@muskalipman.com

This book is dedicated to the Flying Other Brothers
and to my sons, John Paul and Jimi Eric.

Acknowledgments

I want to thank my editor, Dan Foster, for insightful feedback and editing. I also want to thank Mark Abdelnour, technical editor, for useful feedback and many improvements. Danielle Foster and Scribe Tribe worked tirelessly and diligently on page design and composition, and the production team moved heaven and earth to finish this project in record time. Thanks to Kezia Endsley for vigilant proofreading. Also, thanks to the Flying Other Brothers for their music, and band producer Stacy Parrish for tips and wisdom about digital music and iPods.

I owe special thanks to Carole McLendon at Waterside, my agent, for her efforts that went beyond the call of duty, and to Bill Gladstone at Waterside for his support and backing. Finally, thanks to acquisitions editor Kevin Harreld for his patience and direction.

About the Author

Tony Bove has kicked around the computer industry for decades, acting as a pathfinder to new technologies and surprising folks every few years with new projects. He edited the influential newsletter Bove & Rhodes Inside Report on New Media, and wrote weekly and monthly columns and feature articles for computer-industry magazines including *Computer Currents* (for computer users), *Nextworld* (for computer professionals), and *NewMedia* (for multimedia professionals). He also co-founded and edited *Desktop Publishing/Publish* magazine (for publishing professionals).

Tracing the personal computer revolution back to the Sixties counterculture, Tony Bove produced a CD-ROM interactive documentary in 1996, *Haight–Ashbury in the Sixties* (featuring music from the Grateful Dead, Janis Joplin, and the Jefferson Airplane), which garnered critical acclaim and published reviews that refer to it as "An unflinching, nonjudgmental chronicle" (*Wired*), "Inspires then and now connections, fulfilling any historical work's highest calling" (*S.F. Examiner*), "Truly greater than the sum of its parts" (*N.Y. Post*).

Tony Bove has written over a dozen books on computing, desktop publishing, and multimedia, including *The Art of Desktop Publishing* (Bantam); a series of books about Macromedia Director that includes *Macromedia Lingo Studio* and *Official Macromedia Director Studio* (Random House); the long-running *Adobe Illustrator: The Official Handbook for Designers* (Random House), now in its fourth edition; *Desktop Publishing with PageMaker* and *PageMaker 4: The Basics* (John Wiley & Sons); and *The Well-Connected Macintosh* (Harcourt Brace Jovanovich).

Tony Bove has been a director of enterprise marketing for a large software company, as well as a communications director and technical publications manager. He also developed the Rockument music site, www.rockument.com, with commentary and radio programs focused on rock music history. As a founding member of the Flying Other Brothers band (www.flyingotherbros.com), he has performed at numerous benefit concerts and co-written songs with Hot Tuna keyboardist Pete Sears and Saturday Night Live/Bob Dylan bandleader G.E. Smith.

Contents at a Glance

Contents

Chapter 4   **Tweaking the Sound** **113**

Introduction

Eight Days a Week

The iPod arrived at just the right moment. I was about to go on tour with my band, and I wanted to bring music on the road. The songs I wanted to bring were spread out over many different albums from different bands—far too many CDs to carry. I didn't want to burn a new CD of just those songs, because the albums had other songs that we might want to explore. It just seemed like too much guesswork to pre-select the songs I would need.

My first iPod, the 20-gigabyte version, arrived. It could hold more than *8 days* worth of music, if you were to play a different song over the entire 24 hours of each day. (Since then I've added the newer 30-gigabyte version, which holds more than *two weeks* worth of music.)

I didn't realize how convenient the iPod would be until I spent a few days trying to fill it up with music. I ripped CDs as fast as I could, not bothering to select individual songs—entire albums were sucked in, processed, and spit out. Yet I couldn't fill the iPod fast enough.

As I went on tour, it was only about half full, but that was more than enough. Not only could I play songs indefinitely without repeating a song, I also impressed a rock legend I met backstage at one of the shows by pulling out my iPod and playing one of his songs right on the spot. He was so impressed that he autographed my iPod carrying case.

Even the band's sound engineer was impressed. He recorded the entire show that night directly to his Mac-based sound system and then copied the music quickly to my iPod. Ten minutes later, I was back in the tour bus with the night's show on my iPod for everyone to hear.

It's better than a jukebox in your pocket. It's a jukebox you can update.

If you felt the same way I felt when I first got my iPod—like you'd been waiting for something like this—then you may appreciate the approach I took with this book. I started with the premise that it would change your music buying and playing habits forever. Once you start putting music into digital form on your computer, there's no turning back.

Getting digital music *into* an iPod is really quick and easy, especially if you buy the music from the Apple Music Store on the Internet. Organizing the music into playlists takes a little longer, but the task is worth the effort if you want to listen for a long time while driving without having to select songs. Getting music from CDs into the computer (commonly called "ripping") takes only a bit longer than downloading from the Apple Music Store. But selecting the CD, and deciding which songs to play, then putting it into the drive, getting the song titles and information from the Internet, and clicking the button to rip the CD—that whole process takes a bit of time. It's a process you don't want to repeat. You want to get it right the first time.

How This Book Is Organized

This book starts with how to get the best music out of the CD ripping process, so you don't have to do it over again.

Chapter 1 gets you up and running, and you learn right away how to buy music online, rip CDs, and import music from other sources, so that you can fill up your iPod immediately.

Chapter 2 gets you on the road with your iPod, and provides tips on how to use the iPod's controls and how to connect home stereos, portable speakers, headphones, and even car radios to your iPod.

Chapter 3 shows you how to organize your songs and manage your music library on your computer, as well as make backups, create playlists, and update your iPod automatically or manually.

Chapter 4 provides a brief introduction to the world of high-quality digital sound and the specific information you need to refine your CD ripping and importing process to get the best quality music while using the least amount of iPod disk space.

Chapter 5 shows you how to use your iPod as a personal digital assistant (PDA) that can keep track of addresses, phone numbers, calendar appointments, events, and to-do lists.

Chapter 6 gives you total control over your iPod's settings and menus, and shows you how to use it as a hard disk with your computer, copying files and folders, making backups, and saving information for use on the road.

Chapter 7 helps you solve any problems you may have with the iPod and its connection to your computer, including how to reset the iPod, update its firmware, and restore it to its factory settings.

Chapter 1

Getting in Tune

Here's what you'll explore in this chapter:

◆ What you can do with your iPod, with iTunes on a Mac, and with MusicMatch Jukebox on a PC

◆ Buying music from the Apple Music Store, "ripping" audio CDs, and importing music files

◆ Automatically updating your iPod with your music library

Music has changed so much in the transformation to digital that the music industry hardly recognizes it. The benefits to consumers of digital music are so vast that the music industry has been frightened by the transformation, and has held back on allowing music sales over the Internet. Until now.

The Apple iPod music player is the catalyst that has changed the music industry. The iPod is a vast jukebox that you can keep perpetually updated to play the tunes you want to hear. It holds so much music that, no matter how large your music collection, you will seriously consider putting all your music into digital format on your computer, transferring portions of it to the iPod, and playing music from both your computer and from your iPod from now on. You may never stop buying CDs, but you won't have to buy all your music that way. And the music you own will never need to be replaced again.

As a child of the Sixties, this is good news for me. I bought my favorite records at least three, if not four, times—scratchy LPs, fresh copies of LPs, the CD version from the 1980s, and the remixed, re-mastered CD version from the 1990s. Even worse, CDs can become unreliable after 15 years—some I bought in 1985 now have problems with some tracks. This is somewhat infuriating because the quality of the sound on CDs is as good if not better than well-played vinyl records (unless you have a very high quality turntable and a vinyl LP in mint condition). A conspiracy theorist might point out that this situation benefits the record companies, not the consumers. The paranoid might ask how music lovers and consumers could trust an industry that wants to continue to sell you the same music over and over again.

But the solution has come from a technology company—Apple Computer. And although Apple has every right to continue to promote its Macintosh computers as the solution (and for many of us it is much better for organizing music), the company saw the wisdom of making the iPod compatible with Windows PCs. Every iPod now comes with the software you need to make it work with Windows as well as Macintosh OS X.

One considerable benefit of this technology is that you can use your computer as your new digital music library. Put all your music into this library, and you can preserve it forever. Copy as much of it as you want into your iPod, and take it on the road. You can make copies of your music with perfect quality, so no medium that can fail will ever "trap" your music again. The wonderfully remixed, re-mastered, reconstituted version of your favorite album can be copied to a hard disk and managed, just like the rest of your information, so that it never disappears. It never goes away. You never have to buy the same music twice.

You never have to buy the same music twice!

What You Can Do with Your iPod

The iPod is, essentially, a hard disk and a digital music player in one device. The hard disk enables the device to hold far more music than most MP3 players. The 30-gigabyte iPod model can hold around 7,500 songs, depending on how you import them. I use very high quality importing settings, which means that my songs take up much more space than your average MP3 song on the Internet, and yet I've been able to fit, on a 30-gigabyte iPod, more than three weeks' worth of music if played continuously, around the clock—or about one new song a day for the next 20 years.

At 5.6 ounces, the iPod weighs less than two CDs. With an LCD screen, circular scrolling pad, and buttons that feature backlighting for clear visibility in low-light conditions, the iPod is designed for easy one-handed operation. It offers up to 20 minutes of skip protection—twice that of other hard drive-based MP3 players on the market—so you can enjoy outdoor athletic activities without missing a beat. And with a thickness of only 0.62 inches, the iPod fits comfortably in the palm of your hand and slips easily into your pocket.

The iPod is a music player, not a recorder (not yet, anyway). It can update itself automatically to copy your entire music library, if you want. With automatic updating, any changes, additions, or deletions you make in your music library are reflected in your iPod. You also have the option to copy music directly to your iPod, and, with the Mac version, delete music on your iPod and manage updating by playlist.

It takes only about 10 seconds to copy a CD's worth of music to the iPod. The iPod offers high-quality digital music playback and supports the most popular digital audio formats, including MP3 (with MP3 Variable Bit Rate), AIFF, WAV, and the new AAC format, which features CD-quality audio in smaller file sizes than MP3. It also supports the Audible AA spoken word file format. These formats are described in detail in Chapter 4, "Tweaking the Sound."

The iPod is also a "data player," perhaps the first of its kind. As a hard disk, the iPod can serve as a portable backup device for important data files. You can put your calendar and address book on it to help you manage your affairs on the road. While it is not as fully functional as a PDA(there's no keyboard for adding information directly to the device), it is fully functional for viewing the information. Like a PDA, you can keep your calendar and address book automatically synchronized with your computer, where you add and edit information normally.

Whether or not you carry a laptop when traveling, the iPod can be very useful by itself as a convenient information-viewing device (while listening to music, of course). With a laptop, you can keep the iPod up to date as you travel. There's even a sleep timer, so you can fall asleep to your music, and an alarm clock, with which you can choose either an alarm tone or your favorite music to wake you up.

What You Can Do with iTunes (Mac) and MusicMatch Jukebox (PC)

With iTunes for the Mac, or MusicMatch Jukebox for the PC, your computer is a vast jukebox limited only by your disk space, which you could keep perpetually updated to play the tunes you want to hear. You can manage this library and keep a backup copy to preserve the music in high-quality format. iTunes is distributed with every Mac, and the newest version is also available on the CD-ROM that comes with your iPod and on the Apple Web site (www.apple.com) for downloading. The appropriate version of MusicMatch Jukebox licensed by Apple (version 7.50 as of this writing) is available on the CD-ROM supplied with your iPod.

iTunes and MusicMatch Jukebox are very similar in the way they work. It's quick and easy to slip in a CD and "rip" (transfer and digitally encode) songs into your music library. The ripping process is very fast, and track information including artist name and title arrives automatically over the Internet.

It's even quicker and perhaps easier to buy your music online from the Apple Music Store (www.apple.com/music), available just a click away (for Mac users only, as of this writing). iTunes knows how to quickly download music from the store and put it in your library, making the music immediately available for playing, burning onto a CD, or transferring to an iPod.

Both iTunes and MusicMatch Jukebox give you the power to organize songs into playlists and burn CDs of any songs in your library, in any order. With iTunes you can even set up dynamic "smart" playlists that reflect your preferences and listening habits. Both programs offer equalizers with preset settings for all kinds of music and listening environments as well as the ability to customize and save your own settings with each song.

It is fairly simple to connect your computer to a stereo amplifier in your home, or connect speakers to your computer, and use your computer as a smart music "source device" (as in CD player, radio tuner, etc.). iTunes also offers Mac users a music sharing feature that lets you play songs from your music library on any Mac in your house or over the Internet from work to home.

Songs you rip from your CDs and import from Web sites and MP3 repositories can be burned onto another CD, copied to other computers, and transferred to your iPod freely. Songs you buy from the Apple Music Store can be played on up to three computers, burned on up to 10 CDs, and transferred to an iPod. You can even choose which three computers to use—if you switch to a new one, you can "de-authorize" the old one, and your music moves with you.

With these applications, your music is preserved in a high-quality digital format that will always be available to you and never wear out. And you can use this music in different ways. On the Mac, iTunes connects to the rest of iLife, so your entire music library is available to make your iPhoto slideshows, iMovie videos, and iDVD menus rock out. On the PC, you can use your MP3 music files with slideshow and video-editing applications as well as DVD authoring tools.

Setting Up iTunes and MusicMatch Jukebox

Current model Macs come with iTunes already installed, and you can update the version of iTunes you have by using the Software Update option in the System Preferences of Mac OS X. Mac users generally have all of the following, which are required for using an iPod:

- ◆ Mac with built-in FireWire support
- ◆ iTunes 4 or newer
- ◆ Optional: iSync for synchronizing your Address Book and iCal information with the iPod. iSync is available free from Apple at www.apple.com

PC users can install MusicMatch Jukebox from the CD-ROM supplied with the iPod, which is compatible with Windows PCs. You need the following to use the iPod with a PC:

- ◆ A PC with a 300 MHz or faster processor
- ◆ Windows Me, Windows 2000, Windows XP, or newer version of Windows
- ◆ 96 megabytes of RAM (128 megabytes for Windows XP)
- ◆ Built-in or Windows-certified FireWire (IEEE 1394) hardware installed, or USB connection with optional USB-to-iPod-dock cable available from Apple at www.apple.com

The CD-ROM supplied with the iPod automatically starts running when you insert it into a PC (as shown in Figure 1.1), and lets you install the iPod for Windows software (Figure 1.2) as well as MusicMatch Jukebox.

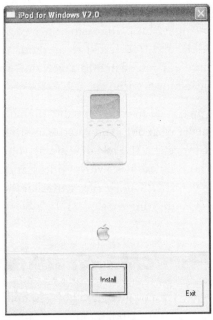

FIGURE 1.1   *The opening screen of the iPod for Windows software.*

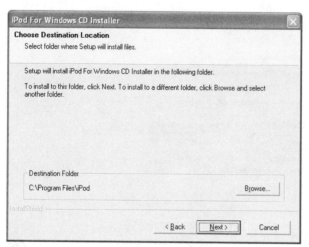

FIGURE 1.2   *Choose the install destination for your iPod for Windows software.*

Starting iTunes (Mac)

When you first start iTunes, the Setup Assistant, shown in Figure 1.3, helps you through the process of setting it up. You need to decide the following two options when you first start iTunes:

◆ **Handle audio content from the Internet, or leave audio settings for the Internet untouched?** Click Yes to allow iTunes to handle Internet audio content. iTunes offers more features than you typically find with browser plug-ins from other companies. On the other hand, if you are happier with your existing plug-ins and helper applications, click No to leave your Internet settings untouched.

◆ **Automatically connect to the Internet, or ask first?** If you use an always-on broadband Internet service, you probably want iTunes to connect automatically, and you should click Yes. If you're using a modem, if your Internet service is intermittently off, or if your Internet service charges when you use it, you probably don't want this connection to be automatic—Click No to set iTunes to ask first.

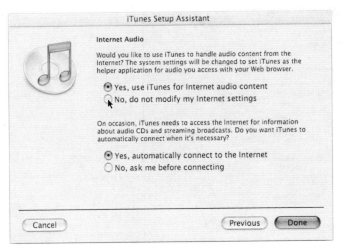

FIGURE 1.3 *Setting up iTunes on a Mac.*

If you have already installed iTunes, the Setup Assistant does not appear and is not needed. Your choices for accessing the Internet are described in more detail in "The Internet and iTunes" in Chapter 3. You can access the iTunes preferences for using the Internet as follows:

1. Choose iTunes>Preferences.
2. Click the General tab in the Preferences window to see the General pane.
3. Turn on or off the "Connect to Internet when needed" option. When on, iTunes connects automatically; when off, iTunes asks first.
4. Click the Set button to use iTunes for Internet music playback.
5. Click OK to close the Preferences window.

Either way, you should at some point connect to the Internet, not only to buy music online and listen to Web radio, but also to retrieve the track information every time you insert an audio CD, so you don't have to type the information yourself.

Setup Assistant also asks if you want iTunes to search your home folder for music files. You may want to click No because iTunes may find files you don't want to add to your library (such as music for games). Setup Assistant also asks if you want to go straight to the Apple Music Store, which you can learn about in "The Apple Music Store" section later in this chapter.

Your next step is to import music from CDs, buy music online, or import music from other sources to build up your music library in iTunes.

Installing and Starting MusicMatch Jukebox (Windows)

Before installing the iPod software for Windows, make sure you are logged in as a Windows Administrator user if you're using Windows 2000 or Windows XP. Quit all other applications before installing, and disable any virus protection software.

If you have installed an earlier version of MusicMatch Jukebox (especially if it is a demo version provided free with your computer), you must use Add/Remove Programs to remove the earlier version before installing the version that came with your iPod. To remove the earlier version, click Start in your Windows taskbar, choose Settings>Control Panels>Add/Remove Programs, and select MusicMatch Jukebox to remove the program(or "uninstall" in some versions of Windows).

 WARNING

When installing the iPod for Windows, be sure your iPod is disconnected from the PC before starting the installation procedure. Wait until the installation software tells you to connect the iPod before connecting your iPod to the PC.

To install the proper software to make your iPod work with Windows, follow these steps *before* connecting your iPod to your PC:

1. Insert the iPod for Windows CD-ROM into your Windows-based PC. Do not connect your iPod to your PC yet.

2. If the installer doesn't open automatically, double-click the CD-ROM icon in the My Computer window, and then double-click the Setup icon.

3. Click Install, and follow the instructions as they appear. iPod for Windows software must be installed on the C: drive in order to work.

4. The installation instructions will tell you when it is time to connect your iPod to the PC. Go ahead and connect it to your PC, and follow the instructions to continue until installation is finished. If the PC doesn't recognize your iPod, see "iPod for Windows Troubleshooting" in Chapter 7.

The iPod will automatically synchronize to your music library when you connect it, but you won't have anything in your music library until you start importing music. Your next step is to import music from CDs, buy music online, or import music from other sources to build up your MusicMatch Jukebox library.

Importing Music

You hold an empty iPod in your hand. It's nice. It has smooth edges and a shiny surface, elegant buttons, and slick connections. It weighs more than you thought it would. It's solid. And yet it's empty.

To get tunes into your iPod, you need to first import the music into iTunes or MusicMatch Jukebox from your audio CDs or other sources, such as online music stores.

The importing process is straightforward, but the settings you choose for importing affect sound quality, disk space (and iPod space), and compatibility with other types of players and computers. Chapter 4 provides an in-depth look at these file formats and quality settings; for now, you can experiment with settings and get some tunes into your iPod right away.

The Apple Music Store

Buying music online is the fastest way to fill your music library, and perhaps the easiest way. The songs are imported automatically without any need to set or change import settings—the songs are pre-encoded in a protected format that is also optimized for fast downloading and high-quality playback in iPods.

 NOTE

As of this writing, the Apple Music Store works only with iTunes on a Mac, but Apple announced that a PC version would be available in a few months, so Windows users may now have the opportunity to use it with MusicMatch Jukebox.

When Apple launched the Apple Music Store on May 2, 2003, the store offered more than 200,000 songs, with most songs costing $0.99 each. The songs are protected for copyright reasons, but you can play the songs on up to three different computers, burn CDs with them, and use them on your iPod. You can preview any song up to 30 seconds, and with an account you can click to buy the song and download it immediately.

To use the Apple Music Store, click Music Store in the Source list (Figure 1.4). Click on the Sign In button on the right, under the Browse button, to create or log in to an account. You need an account (with a credit card) to buy music.

FIGURE 1.4   *Using the Apple Music Store.*

The iTunes song list turns into a browser window with the store's content. You can use the Choose Genre pop-up to go to specific music genres, or click on links to new releases, exclusive tracks, and other store specials.

You may want to listen to a song before buying, or just browse the store by listening to song previews. Each preview is about 30 seconds. When you select an artist or a special offering, the browser window divides and gives you a list of songs you can click on and play, as shown in Figure 1.5.

FIGURE 1.5   *Selecting a song to preview in the Apple Music Store.*

Accompanying each preview is a Buy button that appears at the far right of each song (you may have to scroll your iTunes window horizontally). The previews play on your computer in a stream off the Internet, so there may be a few hiccups in the playback.

With an account set up, you can purchase songs and download them to your computer by clicking the button to buy the song, as shown in Figure 1.6. The store displays a warning to make sure you want to buy the song, as shown in Figure 1.7, and you can either go through with it or cancel. The Apple Music Store offers 1-Click shopping technology that immediately makes the sale and starts the downloading. The song downloads automatically and shows up in your iTunes song list, as shown in Figure 1.8. Purchased songs also appear in a special play list called "Purchased Music" under the Music Store heading as well as in the iTunes Library song list.

FIGURE 1.6   *Clicking the Buy button to buy a song in the Apple Music Store.*

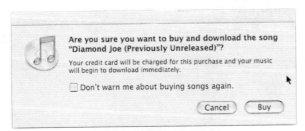

FIGURE 1.7   *The warning that appears before purchasing music from the Apple Music Store.*

FIGURE 1.8   *The song downloads directly from the Apple Music Store into your iTunes Library and appears in your song list.*

 TIP

If for some reason your computer crashes, or you quit before the download is finished, the download will resume when you restart iTunes. If for some reason the download does not continue, choose Advanced>Check For Purchased Music to continue the download.

The first time you set up your account, your computer is "authorized" by Apple to play the songs you buy. When you copy these songs to another computer, you can play them on that computer by providing your ID and password, which authorizes that computer. You can authorize up to three computers total. If you want to use another computer other than the first three you authorize, you can always "de-authorize" one of the first three computers by choosing Advanced>Deauthorize Account.

Once you've set up an account, you can sign in to the music store at any time to buy music, view or change the information in your account, and see your purchase history. To see your account information and purchase history, click the View Account link in the store after signing in with your ID and password. Every time you buy music, you should get an email from the Apple Music Store with the purchase information.

You have a choice of using the 1-Click technology to purchase songs immediately, or adding songs to a shopping cart in the store to delay purchasing and downloading until you are ready. If you have a slow connection to the Internet, you will probably want to use the shopping cart method.

When you use the shopping cart, the buy button for each song says "Add" instead of "Buy." When you're ready to purchase everything in your cart, click Buy Now to close the sale and download all the songs at once.

To switch to the shopping cart method, change your preferences for the Apple Music Store by choosing iTunes>Preferences, then clicking the Store button at the top of the window, as shown in Figure 1.9. The Store preferences window lets you change from 1-Click to Shopping Cart or vice versa. You also have a choice of playing songs after downloading, and loading a complete song preview before playing the preview. This last option provides better playing performance (less hiccups) with previews over slow Internet connections.

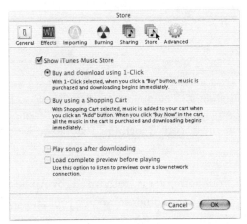

FIGURE 1.9 *Setting your preferences for the Apple Music Store.*

 NOTE

All sales in the Apple Music Store are final. To avoid losing your music if your hard disk crashes, back up your music library as described in Chapter 3. You can also burn your purchased songs onto an audio CD, as described in Chapter 3.

Audio CDs

Importing music from an audio CD takes less time than playing the CD. However, before you actually rip a CD, you should check your importing (recording) settings.

◆ To check your importing settings in iTunes, choose iTunes>Preferences, then click the Importing button at the top of the window, as shown in Figure 1.10.

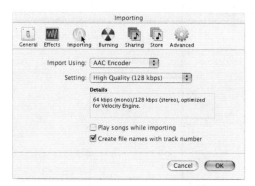

FIGURE 1.10 *Setting your importing prefer-ences for ripping CDs in iTunes.*

◆ To check your importing (called "recorder") settings in MusicMatch Juke-box, choose Options>Settings, and click the Recorder tab. The Recorder pane of the Settings window appears, as shown in Figure 1.11. "Ripping" is slang for the process of compressing the song's digital information and en-coding it in a particular sound file format. Your most important choice is the type of encoding format:

◆ On a Mac, iTunes provides the "Import Using" pop-up menu in the iTunes Importing preferences window.

◆ On a PC, MusicMatch Jukebox provides the "Recording Format" pop-up menu in MusicMatch Jukebox's Recorder settings.

After choosing an encoding format, you can then make changes to its settings, which vary depending on the encoding format you choose.

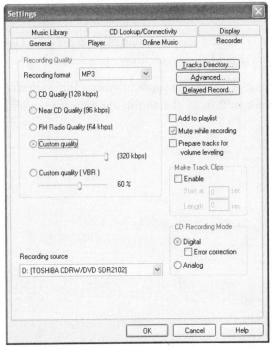

FIGURE 1.11 *Setting your importing (Recorder) settings for ripping CDs in MusicMatch Jukebox.*

Chapter 4 provides a more in-depth look at these choices and settings. For now, you can follow these suggestions:

◆ **AAC Encoder (Mac only):** The format used for songs in the Apple Music Store, recommended for iPods. AAC is excellent for all uses except when ripping your own CDs in order to burn new audio CDs (see AIFF or WAV). Choose High Quality for the Setting pop-up menu, or choose Custom and improve the quality as described in Chapter 4.

◆ **AIFF Encoder (Mac only):** Use AIFF if you plan to burn the song to an audio CD, because it offers the highest possible quality. However, songs encoded in AIFF occupy many times more space than AAC or MP3, and also require more iPod battery power to play. If you use AIFF, choose Automatic for Setting.

◆ **MP3 Encoder:** Supported everywhere—use the MP3 format for songs you intend to send to others over the Internet, or burn an MP3 CD for use with MP3 CD players, or copy to the iPod or other portable MP3 players.

In iTunes, choose Higher Quality for Setting, or choose Custom and improve the quality as we describe in Chapter 4. In MusicMatch Jukebox, choose CD Quality (128 kbps), or choose Custom Quality and move the slider up to 320 kbps (as shown in Figure 1.11).

◆ **WAV Encoder**: WAV is the high-quality sound format used on PCs. However, songs encoded in WAV occupy many times more space than AAC or MP3, and also require more iPod battery power to play. In iTunes, when you use WAV, choose Automatic for Setting. In MusicMatch Jukebox, leave the CD Quality setting as is.

TIP

You can import songs from a CD using one encoder, and then import it again using a different encoder—or simply convert the songs, as described in Chapter 4. For example, you might use AIFF or WAV to encode songs that you intend to burn onto a CD, and then use AAC or MP3 to encode the same songs for use in an iPod. After burning the CD, you could delete the AIFF or WAV versions, which take up a lot of space.

Ripping a CD with iTunes

To rip a CD with iTunes on a Mac, follow these steps:

1. Optional: Choose iTunes>Preferences and click Importing to check or change your import encoder settings. You only have to do this once; iTunes keeps these preferences for importing until you change them. See Chapter 4 to learn all about import settings and encoders. You can skip this step if you are satisfied with your import settings.

2. Insert an audio CD.

   The songs first appear in your song list as generic unnamed tracks. If your computer accesses the Internet at all times, iTunes can connect to the Internet automatically and retrieve the track information every time you insert an audio CD. This only takes a few seconds. If for some reason this didn't happen and you are connected, or you have to connect first by modem, go ahead and establish your connection, then choose Advanced>Get CD Track Names and wait a few seconds.

3. Optional: Click to remove the check mark next to any songs on the CD that you don't want to import.

   iTunes imports the songs that have check marks next to them; when you remove the check mark next to a song, iTunes skips that song.

4. Optional: To remove the gap of silence between songs that segue together, select those songs and choose Advanced>Join CD Tracks.

This happens often with music CDs—the tracks are separate, but the end of one song merges into the beginning of the next song. You don't want an annoying half-second gap between the songs. For example (see Figures 1.12 and 1.13), I joined the first two songs of Sgt. Pepper because, as you probably know, they run together. I also joined the last three songs of the CD for the same reason. To select multiple songs, click on the first one, and then hold down the Command key to click each subsequent song. To select several consecutive songs in a row, click the first one, hold down the Shift key, and click the last one, as shown in Figure 1.12.

5. Click the Import button.

FIGURE 1.12   *Selecting in iTunes a range of songs that have no audible gap between them on the CD.*

FIGURE 1.13   *Joining the songs in iTunes so that there is no audible gap between them when importing.*

The Import button is at the top right edge of the iTunes window. The status display shows the progress of the operation. To cancel, click the small "x" next to the progress bar in the status display.

iTunes plays the songs as it imports them. You can click the pause button to stop playback. You can also turn off the playing of songs automatically by choosing iTunes>Preferences and clicking the Importing button. The Importing preferences window includes the "Play songs while importing" option, which you can turn off.

As iTunes finishes importing each song, it displays a green check mark next to the song, as shown in Figure 1.14. When all the songs are imported, you can eject the CD by clicking the eject button at the far right bottom edge of the iTunes window. You can also choose Controls>Eject Disc to eject the disc.

FIGURE 1.14   *As iTunes finishes importing each song, it displays a green check mark next to the song.*

Ripping a CD with MusicMatch Jukebox

To rip a CD with MusicMatch Jukebox on a Windows PC, follow these steps:

1. Optional: Choose Options>Settings, and click the Recorder tab to check or change your encoder settings. You only have to do this once; MusicMatch Jukebox keeps these settings for recording from audio CD until you change them. See Chapter 4 to learn all about import settings and encoders. You can skip this step if you are satisfied with your import settings.

2. Choose View>Recorder to open the Recorder window, as shown in Figure 1.15.

3. Insert an audio CD.

   The songs first appear in your song list as generic unnamed tracks. If your computer accesses the Internet at all times, MusicMatch Jukebox can connect to the Internet automatically and retrieve the track information every time you insert an audio CD. This only takes a few seconds. If for some reason this didn't happen and you are connected, or you have to connect first by modem, go ahead and establish your connection, and make sure CD Lookup is enabled: choose Options>Settings and click the CD Lookup/Connectivity tab. Then click the Refresh button along the top of the Recorder window.

4. Optional: Click to remove the check mark next to any songs on the CD that you don't want to record (import). MusicMatch Jukebox records the songs that have check marks next to them; when you remove the check mark next to a song, the program skips that song.

5. Click the red Record button on the recorder to start importing the music.

6. Watch MusicMatch Jukebox rip the CD. When it's done, the program automatically ejects the CD.

During recording, the status display shows the progress of the operation. To cancel, click the Cancel button in the Recorder window.

FIGURE 1.15   *Recording songs from an audio CD using MusicMatch Jukebox.*

Music from Other Sources

You can bring music from any source into either the iTunes or MusicMatch Jukebox libraries, and from the music library into your iPod. Music can be imported from any source—it's mostly a question of high fidelity.

◆ **Internet:** You can import MP3 tunes from Web sites by first downloading the MP3 files. You can also link your Mac or PC to Web radio stations, but you can't capture the songs from Web broadcasts without special software. The quality of the music depends on the quality of the source. Web sites and services offering MP3 files vary widely.

◆ **Professional editing programs:** You can import high-quality AIFF or WAV files from sound editing programs such as Digidesign Pro Tools.

◆ **Any analog source:** You can record music directly into a digital file. On a Mac, you can use the Mac's line-in connector and the Sound Studio program, found in the Applications folder in Mac OS X systems. (You can use it for about 2 weeks before paying for it.) On a PC you can use the line-in connector on your sound card, and the Record Line-In function in MusicMatch Jukebox. On both PCs and Macs, you can connect any music source to the line-in connector, including home stereos with turntables for playing vinyl records, or even a microphone for recording live directly into the computer.

Importing to iTunes

Once you've saved, or copied, an MP3, AIFF, or WAV file on your hard disk, you can simply drag it into the iTunes window to import it to your library, as shown in Figure 1.16. If you drag a folder or disk icon, all the audio files it contains are added to your iTunes Library.

FIGURE 1.16   *Dragging an MP3 file into iTunes to import it.*

When you drag a song to your iTunes Library, a copy is placed inside the iTunes Music Folder. The original is not changed or moved. You can then convert the song to another format—for example, you can convert an AIFF file to an MP3 file, while leaving the original intact. I describe converting songs in Chapter 4.

Importing to MusicMatch Jukebox

Once you've saved, or copied, an MP3 or WAV file on your hard disk, click the Add (+) button in the MusicMatch Jukebox Library window. You can then browse your hard disk to find folders of music, and either add music files separately, or add entire folders of files at once.

You can also direct MusicMatch Jukebox to search your hard drive for music to add to your library. Choose Options>Music Library>Search and Add Tracks From All Drives. You can use this function to import music from a network server as well as from your own hard disks.

Audible Books and Voice Recordings (Mac Only)

Do you like to listen to audio books and spoken magazine and newspaper articles? Not only can you bring these sounds into iTunes, but you can also transfer them to your iPod and take them on the road, which is much more convenient than taking cassettes or CDs.

Audible is a leading provider of downloadable spoken audio files. Audible lets you enable up to three computers to play the audio files, just like the Apple Music Store. You can't add Audible files to a fourth computer unless you disable your account on one of the first three computers.

To import Audible files, follow these steps:

1. Go to www.audible.com and set up an account if you don't already have one.
2. Choose and download an Audible audio file. These are files whose names end with ".aa."
3. Drag the Audible file to the iTunes window.

If this is the first time you've added an Audible file, iTunes asks for your account information. You need only enter this information once for each computer you use with your Audible account.

To disable an Audible account, open iTunes on the computer that will no longer use the account, and choose Advanced>Deauthorize Computer, then choose the option to "deauthorize" the computer for the Audible account.

Setting Up Your iPod

The box in which your iPod came includes everything you need to use the iPod with a Mac. To use it with a PC, you need either a FireWire (IEEE 1394) connection, or a USB connection with the optional USB-to-dock cable (optional, purchased separately).

The box includes a CD-ROM with the iTunes software for the Mac, and MusicMatch Jukebox and iPod for Windows for the PC. It also includes the cables you need to connect either the iPod itself or its dock to a FireWire connection.

- ◆ Current models offer a dock and a special cable to connect the dock to the Mac's FireWire connection.
- ◆ Older models offer a FireWire cable for connecting the iPod's FireWire connection to the Mac's FireWire connection.

All models come with a FireWire-compatible power adapter for connecting either the older iPod or the newer iPod-in-dock to an AC power source.

You also get a set of portable earphones and a "remote" controller that connects to the iPod by wire. The accessories don't stop there—you may also have a carrying case and some other goodies. Apple also provides a long list of optional accessories at www.apple.com.

You also need a few things outside the box:

- ◆ **Computer:** Either a Mac with a built-in FireWire port, running Mac OS X version 10.1.4 or newer; or a 300 MHz or faster PC with at least 96 MB of RAM running Windows Me, 2000, or XP (with at least 128 MB of RAM), and a built-in or Windows-certified IEEE 1394 (FireWire) or a USB connection.
- ◆ **Software:** You need to install iTunes 4.0 or newer (provided on CD-ROM with the iPod, or downloaded directly from Apple through Software Update in the System Preferences). For PCs, you need to install MusicMatch Jukebox 7.5 or newer, also included on the CD-ROM.

◆ **Optional Software for Mac users:** You should install iSync, a free utility program from Apple for synchronizing your iPod with your address book and calendar, and iCal for creating and editing your calendar. Both are available for free downloading from www.apple.com.

Powering Your iPod

The iPod's battery lasts about 8 hours, according to Apple's documentation and our experiments, and it recharges automatically when you connect the iPod to a power source. That power source can be either the power adapter supplied with the iPod, or a computer connected by FireWire cable.

Older iPod models offer a Mac-like FireWire connection on the top of the iPod, but newer models use instead a dock that connects to the iPod and offers FireWire and USB to various devices, and a line-out connection for connecting your home stereo. The dock includes a cable with a dock connector on one end and a FireWire (or optional USB) connector on the other, as shown in Figure 1.17.

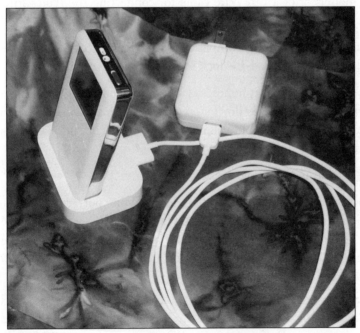

FIGURE 1.17 *The iPod in its dock, connected to the Apple power adapter.*

You can connect the FireWire end to the power adapter to charge the iPod's battery. You can also connect the FireWire end to the computer for synchronizing with your music library, or in the case of iTunes on the Mac, updating the iPod or playing the iPod's songs through the Mac. The FireWire connection provides power to the iPod as long as the computer is not in sleep mode.

The iPod's battery is internal and not removable—it was designed to last as long as the iPod itself. Use only the power adapter supplied with the iPod. It takes about an hour to charge the battery to about 80 percent, and 4 hours to charge it fully. If your iPod is inactive for 28 days, you must recharge its battery.

 NOTE

You should not keep the iPod encased in its carrying case when charging, as it may damage the iPod. Remove it from its case first. It is not unusual for the bottom of the case of the iPod to get warm while it is on—the bottom functions as a cooling surface that transfers heat from inside the unit to the cooler air outside.

A battery icon in the top-right corner of the iPod's display indicates with a progress bar how much power is left—if the icon does not animate, it means the battery is fully charged. When you're charging the battery, the icon turns into a lightning bolt inside a battery. You can disconnect the iPod and use it before the battery is fully charged.

Setting the Language

If your iPod is set to a language other than one you know, you can fix it without having to know the language. To set the language, no matter what language the menu is using, follow these steps:

1. Press the Menu button until pressing it does not change the words on the display. When the Menu button no longer changes the display, it means you are at the main menu.
2. In the main iPod menu, pick the fourth item from the top (it should be Settings in English).
3. In the Settings menu, pick the sixth item from the top (it should be Language).
4. Pick the language. English is at the top of the list.

If the above steps don't work, the iPod's main menu may have been customized (described in Chapter 6). You can reset all of the iPod's settings to bring the iPod back to its original state. Follow these steps to reset all your settings, no matter what language is displayed:

1. Press the Menu button until pressing it does not change the words on the display.
2. In the main menu, pick the fourth item from the top (it should be Settings in English).
3. In the Settings menu, pick the last item at the bottom of the menu (it should be Reset All Settings).
4. Select the second menu item (it should be Reset), and select a language.

The language you choose is subsequently used for all the iPod's menus.

Connecting to Your Computer

Depending on your iPod model, your cable either connects directly to your iPod (older models), or to a dock. If you're already using the cable to charge up your iPod, you can disconnect if from the power adapter and connect that same end to the FireWire connection on your Mac or PC. In fact, you could leave your dock connected to your computer in this fashion and use the computer to charge up the iPod's battery through the FireWire connection.

Connecting to a Mac

Mac users have a FireWire connection on their Macs marked by a radioactive-looking Y symbol. The cable supplied with your iPod has a six-pin connector that inserts into your Mac's FireWire connection.

When you first connect the iPod to a Mac, the iTunes Setup Assistant appears as shown in Figure 1.18. You can give your iPod a name, which is a good idea if you plan on sharing several iPods among several computers.

In the Setup Assistant, you can also turn on or off the option to automatically update your iPod. If this is your first time using an iPod, you probably want to fill it up right away, so leave this option on. If you want to copy only a portion of your library to the iPod, turn this option off, and read "iPod Updating Options" in Chapter 3 for instructions on how to copy music directly.

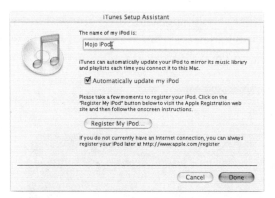

FIGURE 1.18   *Setting up the iPod for use with a Mac.*

After clicking Done in the Setup Assistant, the iPod's name appears in the iTunes Source list near the top. If you have automatic update turned on, the iPod's name appears grayed out, and you can't open it. If you have automatic update turned off, the iPod's name appears just like any other source in the Source list, and you can open it and play songs on the iPod through iTunes and your Mac speakers.

The iPod's icon also appears on the Finder desktop. If you leave your iPod connected to the Mac, it will appear on the desktop and in iTunes whenever you start iTunes.

TIP

To see how much free space remains on your iPod, you can use the Mac Finder. Select the iPod icon on the Finder desktop, and choose File>Show Info. To see how much free space is left on the iPod using just the iPod, use the About command in the iPod's Settings menu: choose Main menu>Settings>About.

Connecting to a PC

PC users have either a USB connection, or a FireWire card or connection. An adapter is provided in the iPod box for PC-type FireWire (IEEE 1394) connections.

When you first connect the iPod to a PC, during the installation process, the iPod should be properly configured to run. The iPod for Windows software should automatically run MusicMatch Jukebox when it detects the iPod. If the program does not automatically run, you can launch it yourself by double-clicking the icon for MusicMatch Jukebox. (If you have problems getting your PC to recognize the iPod, see Chapter 7, which contains helpful troubleshooting tips.)

In MusicMatch Jukebox, your iPod should appear in the PortablesPlus window under the Attached Portable Devices folder, as shown in Figure 1.19. If the window is not yet open, choose File>Send to Portable Device.

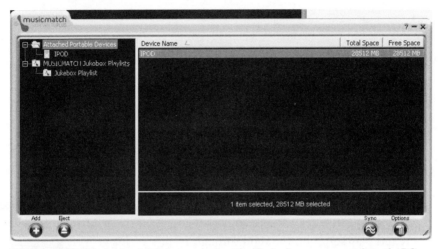

FIGURE 1.19 *MusicMatch Jukebox recognizes the iPod when you connect it to the PC, and adds it to the list of portable devices in the PortablesPlus window.*

Updating Your iPod Automatically

Before you add music to your iPod, you need to import the music into iTunes or MusicMatch Jukebox on your computer. As you build up your music library on your computer, you can update your iPod at any time to copy the music you imported, keeping your iPod up-to-date with your music library. Adding music to your iPod, and deleting music from your iPod, can be completely automatic. By default, your iPod is set up to update itself automatically, synchronizing itself with your music library.

When your iPod updates itself automatically, it matches your library exactly, song for song, playlist for playlist. iTunes or MusicMatch Jukebox automatically copies everything in your music library to the iPod, but does not copy songs stored remotely (such as songs shared from other iTunes libraries on a network). If you made changes in your music library after the last time you updated your iPod, those changes are automatically made in the iPod when you connect it again to your computer. If you added or deleted songs in your library, those songs are likewise added or deleted in your iPod's library.

You can update your iPod in other ways, and you can copy music directly to the iPod, as described in "iPod Updating Options" in Chapter 3. If you are starting up a music library for the first time, you will probably want to update the iPod automatically.

Mac Automatic Update

Mac iTunes users, follow these steps:

1. Connect the iPod to your Mac.

   When you connect the iPod to the Mac, the first thing it does is automatically update itself with your music library—unless you turned off the "automatic update" option in the Setup Assistant or changed the update options as described in Chapter 3.

2. When the update is complete, click the iPod Eject button, or drag the iPod's icon on the Finder desktop to the trash.

When the updating is finished, the iTunes status view says "iPod update is Complete"—you can then click the iPod Eject button, which appears in the bottom right side of the iTunes window, replacing the CD Eject button. You can also "eject" (same as "un-mount") the iPod by dragging the iPod's icon on the Finder's desktop to the trashcan. After you drag it to the trashcan, the iPod display says that it is "OK to disconnect," and you can then disconnect your iPod from its dock, or disconnect the dock from your computer.

PC Automatic Update

PC MusicMatch Jukebox users, follow these steps:

1. Connect your iPod to your PC and wait for it to be recognized by MusicMatch Jukebox. Your iPod should appear in the PortablesPlus window under the Attached Portable Devices folder, as shown in Figure 1.19. If the window is not yet open, choose File>Send to Portable Device.

2. Click the Options button, then the Synchronization tab, and choose the Complete Library Synchronization option, as shown in Figure 1.20.

3. Click the Sync button to update the iPod with your MusicMatch Jukebox music library. The PortablesPlus window displays a warning message, as shown in Figure 1.21. Click Yes to continue.

4. When the synchronization is completed (Figure 1.22), click the Eject button at the bottom-left side of the PortablesPlus window to eject the iPod.

FIGURE 1.20 *Setting your iPod to synchronize its library with yourMusicMatch Jukebox music library, making the iPod an exact duplicate.*

FIGURE 1.21 *MusicMatch Jukebox warns you before updating your iPod with its music library, so that you can cancel if you want.*

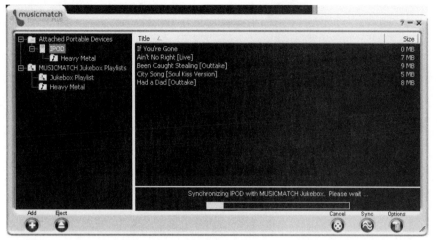

FIGURE 1.22 *After clicking Yes, MusicMatch Jukebox updates your iPod with its music library.*

 NOTE

While updating, your iPod displays the warning: "Do not disconnect." Wait for the update to finish before clicking the Eject button in the PortablesPlus window to eject (un-mount) the iPod. Then, wait for the iPod to display the message "OK to disconnect" before disconnecting it from your computer. See "Un-Mounting (Ejecting) the iPod" in Chapter 6 for detailed instructions on how to "unmount" the iPod.

Now you're in tune; you've got music in your iPod! You're ready to go mobile with your iPod. Chapter 2 has arrived just in time to help you learn how to rock out.

Chapter 2

Going Mobile

Here's what you'll explore in this chapter:

◆ Using the iPod's scroll pad and buttons to play music

◆ Repeating and shuffling songs and albums for playback, and defining an "On-The-Go" playlist

◆ Connecting your iPod to home stereo systems, portable stereos and speakers, headphones, and car accessories

◆ Controlling the sound quality with the iPod's equalizer presets

The iPod is designed to play music right in your hand, while you move about the world—hiking, jogging, driving a car, riding in a boat, and so on. It offers all the features of high-quality music, but not just for home stereos in living rooms. You can leave your CDs at home and take your music with you, connecting your iPod to everything from portable stereos to headphones to car tape decks to tiny battery-powered portable speakers. You can even use it with an old-fashioned car radio.

The iPod can provide high-quality music no matter how rough the ride. Although the iPod is essentially a hard disk, it also has a 32 MB memory cache made up of solid-state memory, with no mechanical or moving parts, so movement doesn't affect playback. Skip protection works by preloading up to 20 minutes of music to the cache at a time. The iPod plays music from its memory cache rather than the hard disk, so even rigorous activities won't cause music to skip.

This chapter explains how to connect your iPod to a variety of different speaker systems and use your iPod in different listening environments. It also offers a summary of accessories, such as headphones, power cables, and connection cables and devices, which together enable you to use the iPod just about anywhere.

Playing Music on the iPod

Apple designed the iPod to be held in one hand with simple operations performed by your thumb. It offers a unique circular scrolling pad that makes scrolling through an entire music collection quick and easy. The buttons above the scrolling pad (or arranged around the pad in older models) perform simple functions with a single press. The button at the center of the scrolling pad selects items in each menu.

To play a song, first select a song, album, or playlist by scrolling with the pad until it is highlighted, then click the Play/Pause button or the center button in the pad.

Thumbing Through the Menus

The iPod's menu starts out with five selections, as shown in Figure 2.1.

- ◆ **Playlists:** Select a playlist to play.
- ◆ **Browse:** Select by artist, album, song, genre, or composer.
- ◆ **Extras:** View and set the clock and alarm clock, view contacts, view your calendar, view notes, and play games.
- ◆ **Settings:** Set display settings, menu settings, the backlight timer, the equalizer, the date and time, the language, shuffle and repeat modes, the clicker, and the method of sorting your contacts.
- ◆ **Backlight:** Turn on or off the backlighting for your iPod display.

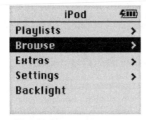

FIGURE 2.1   *The iPod main menu.*

The iPod's main menu is the gateway to all of its functions. This menu can be customized to include additional items (as described in Chapter 6), so your friend's iPod might have more items in the main menu.

Using the Buttons

Your iPod's buttons do the following:

- ◆ **Previous/Rewind:** Start a song over. Press twice to skip to the previous song. Press and hold to rewind through a song.

◆ **Menu:** Go back to the previous menu. (If a song is playing, it continues to play while you check the menu.) Press and hold the Menu button to turn on the backlight.

◆ **Play/Pause:** Play the selected song, selected album, or playlist. Click Play/Pause when a song is playing to pause (stop) the playback.

◆ **Next/Fast-Forward:** Skip to the next song. Press and hold Next/Fast-Forward to fast-forward through the song.

When used in combination, the scroll pad and buttons can perform more complex functions:

◆ **Turn iPod on:** Press any button.

◆ **Turn iPod off:** Press and hold the Play/Pause button.

◆ **Stop playing a song:** Press the Play/Pause button while a song is playing.

◆ **Disable the iPod's buttons:** Set the Hold switch to Hold. (An orange bar appears on one side of the switch.) Set the Hold switch to Hold to avoid unintended functions caused by accidentally pressing the buttons.

◆ **Enable the iPod's buttons:** Set the Hold switch to normal. (The orange bar on one side of the switch is covered over.)

◆ **Reset the iPod:** Set the Hold switch to Hold, then back to normal (off Hold). Then press the Menu and Play/Pause buttons simultaneously for about 5 seconds, until the Apple logo appears in the iPod display.

◆ **Turn Backlight on and off:** Press and hold the Menu button (or select Backlight from the main menu).

◆ **Change the volume:** After starting to play a song (the display says "Now Playing"), use the scroll pad to adjust the volume.

◆ **Skip to any point in a song:** After starting to play a song (the display says "Now Playing"), press the Select button (the center button in the pad); then use the scroll pad to scroll to any point in the song.

Repeating and Shuffling Songs

Your iPod can perform like a CD player, allowing you to repeat the same song or repeat a sequence of songs. You can also *shuffle* (play in random order) songs within an album or playlist, or any songs in your library.

To set your iPod to repeat a single song:

1. Select and play song on your iPod. (To play a song, first select a song, album, or playlist by scrolling with the pad until it is highlighted, then click the Play/Pause button or the center button in the pad.)

2. Choose Settings>Repeat from the iPod's main menu while the song is playing.

3. Press Select (the center button) once, for One, to repeat one song.

To set your iPod to repeat all the songs in the selected album or playlist:

1. Select an album or playlist on your iPod and start playing a song in the album or playlist. If you don't select an album or playlist first, the iPod repeats the entire song list.

2. Choose Settings>Repeat from the iPod's main menu.

3. Press Select (the center button) twice, for All, to repeat all the songs in the selected album or playlist.

Shuffling is playing songs in a random order. To set your iPod to shuffle songs within an album or playlist:

1. Select an album or playlist on your iPod start playing a song in the album or playlist. If you don't select an album or playlist first, the iPod shuffles the playing order of the entire song list.

2. Choose Settings>Shuffle from the iPod's main menu.

3. Press Select (the center button) once, for Songs, to shuffle the songs in the selected album or playlist.

To set your iPod to shuffle albums while still playing the songs in each album in normal album order:

1. Select an album or playlist on your iPod start playing a song in the album or playlist.

2. Choose Settings>Shuffle from the iPod's main menu.

3. Press Select (the center button) twice, for Albums, to shuffle the albums without shuffling the songs within each album.

When your iPod is set to shuffle, it won't repeat a song until it has played through the entire album, playlist, or library.

On-The-Go Playlist

You can pre-select a playlist of songs so that you can do other things (such as driving) without having to use the iPod's buttons and scroll pad. If you created playlists in iTunes or MusicMatch Jukebox, those playlists appear in the Playlists menu.

If you haven't yet created playlists, or you want to create a temporary playlist, you can do so right on your iPod by selecting a list of songs or entire albums to play in a certain order. Queued songs appear automatically in a playlist called "On-The-Go" in the Playlists menu.

To select songs or entire albums for your On-The-Go playlist:

1. Highlight a song or album title.
2. Press and hold the Select button (the center button on the scroll pad) until the title flashes.
3. Repeat steps 1 and 2 in the order you want the songs or albums played.

To play your On-The-Go playlist, choose Playlists>On-The-Go to view your list, as shown in Figure 2.2. Highlight the first (or any) title in the list, and press the Play button (or the Select button) to play.

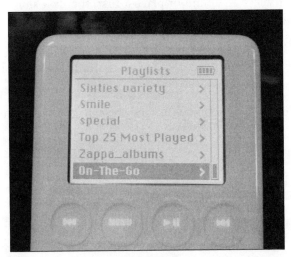

FIGURE 2.2 *Selecting the On-The-Go playlist, which is the last playlist in the list displayed after choosing Playlists from the main menu.*

The iPod saves your On-The-Go playlist so that you can repeat it or hear it some other time. To clear the On-The-Go playlist, select Playlists>On-The-Go>Clear Playlist.

Adjusting the Volume

The iPod can be quite loud through your headphones, and too loud for stereo speakers, if it is set to its highest volume. For best results and least distortion, you should keep the volume to about half of its possible range.

To adjust the volume, select and play a song on your iPod, and while the song is playing, use the scroll pad: Scroll with your thumb or finger clockwise to increase the volume, and counter-clockwise to decrease the volume. A volume bar appears in the iPod's display to guide you.

If you have the Apple iPod Remote that connects to the top of your iPod, you can control the volume using the Volume button on the remote. Use the remote to adjust the volume, play or pause a song, fast-forward or rewind, and skip to the next or previous song. You can also disable the buttons on the remote by setting the remote's Hold switch. The remote comes in handy when you're driving or using your iPod with stereo speakers or a home stereo system.

Making iPod Connections

Small but versatile, the iPod can connect to any separately powered stereo system or headphones, and to FireWire-equipped computers, to play music stored on the iPod.

The iPod's connections, as shown in Figure 2.3 (current models) and Figure 2.4 (older models), are as follows:

- ◆ **FireWire:** New models have a dock connection on the bottom. The dock includes a cable with a dock connector on one end and a FireWire (or optional USB) connector on the other. Older iPods have a Mac-style FireWire connection on the top that works with any standard Mac FireWire cable.
- ◆ **Headphone out (with control socket):** The combination headphone and control socket connection lets you plug in the Apple iPod Remote, which in turn provides a headphone out. The remote control offers playback and volume control buttons. You can connect headphones or a 3.5-millimeter stereo mini-plug cable, to the headphone out.

◆ **Dock connection:** The iPod's dock offers two connections—one for the special cable for FireWire (or USB) connections, and a line-out connection for a stereo mini-plug cable (or headphones).

Connect the dock's FireWire cable to your computer (for synchronizing, updating, and playing music through the computer's speakers) or to the power adapter to charge the iPod's battery. The FireWire connection provides power to your iPod as long as your computer is not in sleep mode.

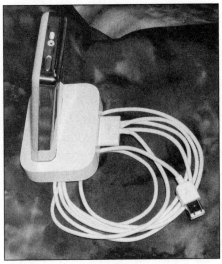

FIGURE 2.3   *Current model 30-gigabyte iPod with its dock.*

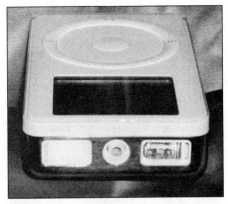

FIGURE 2.4   *Older model 20-gigabyte iPod with connections on top.*

Home and Portable Stereo Systems

Home stereo systems come in many shapes and sizes, but one thing common to stereo systems is the ability to add another input device, such as a portable CD player. You need to locate the component of the stereo system that accepts "line-level" input. In expensive stereo systems, the component is typically the preamplifier, amplifier, or tuner. Less expensive stereos and boom boxes are all one piece, but you should find connections somewhere on the device for audio input. There should also be a switch or knob for selecting different input sources, such as CD, Phono, Tuner, Tape, Video, and AUX. Most likely, you can use the AUX, Tape, or Video inputs and get excellent high-quality sound from your iPod.

 WARNING

Do *not* use Phono (for phonograph, a.k.a. turntable) input (labeled "PHONO IN" on most stereos). Phono uses a higher gain level. You might get a loud buzzing sound if you do this, which could damage your speakers. Always lower the master volume control before connecting an input source such as the iPod, and then raise the volume as you start playing music.

Most stereos let you connect an input device using RCA-type cables—one (typically marked red) for the right channel, and one for the left channel. All you need is a cable with a stereo mini-plug on one end and RCA-type connectors on the other, as shown in Figure 2.5. (Stereo mini-plugs have two black bands on the tip of the plug, while a mono mini-plug has only one black band.)

I recommend Monster's high-performance, dual "balanced" iCable for iPod, available in the Apple Store; any good-quality shielded cables found at a consumer electronics store work fine.

Connect the stereo mini-plug cable to the iPod dock's line-out connection, which offers a better signal for home stereos than the headphone connection. (For iPods without docks, use the headphone connection at the top of the iPod.) Connect the left and right RCA-type connectors to the stereo system's audio input—for example, AUX IN for auxiliary input, or TAPE IN for tape deck input, or CD IN for CD player input.

Volume can sometimes change dramatically from one source (CD player, Tape, iPod, etc.) to another. It is a good idea always to begin with stereo volume controls

FIGURE 2.5 *RCA right (red) and left connectors and a stereo mini-plug (bottom), along with a portable speaker system and its stereo mini-plug.*

adjusted to minimum when first beginning to play music from a new source. Turn up the volume control to the desired level after you've begun playing music from the new source.

You can control the volume from the iPod using the scroll pad while a song is playing: scrolling clockwise turns the volume up, and counter-clockwise turns it down. This controls the volume of the signal from the iPod. Stereo systems typically have their own volume control to raise or lower the volume of the amplified speakers. For optimal sound quality when using a home stereo, set the iPod volume at less than half the maximum output and adjust your listening volume through your stereo controls. This prevents over-amplification, which can cause distortion and reduce audio quality.

Headphones and Hard-Wired Portable Speakers

Apple designed the iPod to provide excellent sound through headphones, and through the headphone connection the iPod can also serve music to hard-wired speaker systems. The speaker system must be self-powered (with its own amplifier) and must allow audio to be input through a 3.5-millimeter stereo connection.

The iPod has a powerful 60-milliwatt amplifier to deliver audio signals through its headphone connection. It has a frequency response of 20 Hz to 20 kHz, which provides distortion-free music from the lowest to highest frequencies.

Apple supplies excellent ear bud-style headphones with tiny ear buds that fit inside your ear. The ear bud-style headphones rely on neodymium transducers, a rare earth magnet that significantly enhances frequency response and overall sound quality. Most other headphones use aluminum, cobalt, or ceramic drivers; at the same size, the neodymium driver is five times as powerful, increasing the accuracy of the sound and minimizing distortion.

Hard-wired speaker systems, such as the Sony SRS-T77 portable speaker system shown in Figure 2.5 (battery-powered and no larger than your hand), typically offer a stereo mini-plug you can attach directly to the iPod's headphone connection or the dock line-out connection. To place the speakers farther away from the iPod, you can use a stereo mini-plug extension cable (available at most consumer electronics stores), which has a stereo mini-plug on one end and a stereo mini-socket on the other.

Some hard-wired speaker systems have volume controls to raise or lower the volume. For optimal sound quality when using a hard-wired speaker system, set the iPod volume at less than half the maximum output and adjust your listening volume through your speaker system controls. This prevents over-amplification, which can cause distortion and reduce audio quality.

Playing Music on Your Mac

You can play the iPod's music directly on a Mac, through the Mac's speakers and through the headphone connection, using iTunes. This can come in handy—for example, if you wanted to use someone else's Mac (perhaps even a publicly accessible Mac at a copy shop or coffeehouse) to play the music on your iPod through the Mac's speakers. You can't copy songs from the iPod to the other computer directly, but you can easily play the songs on your iPod.

Depending on your Mac model, you may already have excellent speakers. As of this writing, the iMac (with the round base and "office-lamp" monitor) includes semi-globe shaped speakers that perform very well. And Apple designed Macs with connections for adding your own speakers.

Normally, when you connect your iPod to your Mac, iTunes starts up and automatically updates the iPod with your iTunes music library (unless you turned off the "automatic update" option in the Setup Assistant or changed it with the iPod button for iPod options). To play music from your iPod through your Mac, follow these steps:

1. Select the iPod in the iTunes Source list. Your iPod's name appears in the iTunes Source list near the top.

2. Click the iPod Options button. The iPod Options button is on the bottom-right side of the iTunes window, to the left of the Equalizer button.

3. Turn on the "Manually manage songs and playlists" option by clicking the check box next to the option (as shown in Figure 2.6).

FIGURE 2.6   *Setting the option to manage songs manually on the iPod.*

After turning this option on, iTunes displays the message, "Disabling automatic update requires manually unmounting the iPod before each disconnect." It means that when you're finished playing music, you will have to drag the iPod's icon on the Finder's desktop to the trash, or use the iPod eject button to eject the iPod. See "Un-mounting (Ejecting) the iPod" in Chapter 6 for more information about using the iPod as a disk and un-mounting the iPod.

After setting the iPod to update manually, your iPod's name appears in full black and its song list appears when you select it. The iPod name can be opened like any other iTunes source in the list, as shown in Figure 2.7. You can then use Browse to browse the list, as shown in Figure 2.8, or play any playlist.

To connect to a *different* Mac than your own and play your iPod's music, follow the same steps. However, when you connect your iPod to a different Mac, iTunes starts

FIGURE 2.7   *Opening the iPod's playlists in iTunes.*

FIGURE 2.8   *Clicking the Browse button to browse the iPod's library in iTunes.*

up and displays the message, "This iPod is linked to another iTunes music library. Do you want to change the link to this iTunes music library and replace all existing songs and playlists on this iPod with those from this library?" If you just want to play the songs on your iPod and don't want to change your iPod to have this other music library, click the No button, as shown in Figure 2.9.

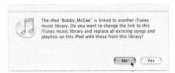

FIGURE 2.9 *The warning you get when you use your iPod with another computer. Click No to keep your iPod's music library intact.*

 WARNING

If you click Yes for the music library question displayed by iTunes on computers other than your own, the music library on your iPod will be deleted and iTunes will update your iPod with the library from that computer. If you use a public computer with no music in its library, this action will delete all the music in your iPod. If you use a friend's computer, your friend's music library will be copied to your iPod, deleting the music that was previously in your iPod.

Playing Music on Your PC

You can play the iPod's music directly on your PC using MusicMatch Jukebox and listen through the PC's speakers or headphone/line-out connection. This can come in handy—for example, if you wanted to use someone else's PC to play the music on your iPod through the PC's speakers. You can't copy songs from the iPod to the other computer directly, but you can easily play the songs on your iPod, and you can copy music *to* the iPod.

Normally, when you connect your iPod to your Windows-based PC, MusicMatch Jukebox starts up and displays the iPod in the PortablesPlus window. To play music from your iPod through your PC, follow these steps:

1. Connect your iPod to the PC, as described in Chapter 1. Wait a few minutes for the iPod to be recognized by MusicMatch Jukebox. Your iPod should appear in the PortablesPlus window under the Attached Portable Devices folder. If the window is not yet open, choose File>Send to Portable Device to open it.

2. When your iPod appears in the PortablesPlus window in the column on the left side, select it. The iPod music library appears in the right side of the PortablesPlus window, as shown in Figure 2.10.

3. Select one or more songs in the iPod Library in the PortablesPlus window. To select a range of songs, click on the first song, and then hold down the Shift key while clicking on the last song. To add single songs to your selection, hold down the Control key while clicking on them. You can also select an iPod playlist to show only the playlist songs in the right side of the PortablesPlus window, for easier song selection. Select a playlist by clicking the + sign next to the iPod to display the playlists on the iPod, and select a playlist to see its contents.

4. Drag the selected songs into the MusicMatch Jukebox playlist window, as shown in Figure 2.10. The order of songs in the playlist is based on the order in which you selected and dragged them to the list.

5. The first song in the playlist should automatically start playing. You can control song playback with MusicMatch Jukebox's Play, Stop, Pause, Next, and Previous buttons.

FIGURE 2.10 *Using the playlist window in MusicMatch Jukebox to play songs on the iPod through the PC and the PC's speakers.*

Listening to iPod Music on the Road

You have an entire music library in a device that fits in your shirt pocket. You can take it anywhere and play music anywhere. If you can't plug your iPod into power while playing, its battery will provide up to 10 hours of playing time before you need to recharge it. With skip protection, you don't have to worry about turbulence, potholes, or strenuous exercise causing the music to skip.

Bring along an extra pair of headphones or ear buds and a splitter cable, like the one in Figure 2.11 (available in any consumer electronics store) or the Monster iSplitter (available in the Apple Store). You can use it to plug two pairs of headphones into your iPod and share your music with someone on the road. You can find many iPod accessories useful for traveling in the Apple Store at www.apple.com.

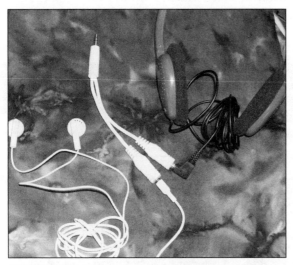

FIGURE 2.11 *A 3.5-millimeter splitter cable for connecting two sets of headphones.*

Car Accessories

To play your iPod in a car, you need an auto-charger to save on battery power and a way to connect to your car's stereo system.

The auto-chargers for older iPods provide a FireWire connector, while the auto-charger for the new dockable iPods use a dock connector cable. In the Apple Store, you can find an auto-charger from Belkin with the appropriate FireWire-to-dock connector cable, shown in Figure 2.12. It offers a convenient socket for a stereo mini-plug cable, which can connect directly to stereos that include a mini-socket for audio input.

Connecting to the car stereo is more difficult. Not many car stereos offer a mini-socket for audio input. But you can use either a cassette player-adapter to connect with your car stereo, or a wireless device described in the next section.

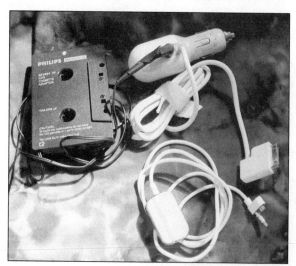

FIGURE 2.12   *Accessories for playing in cars: cassette-player adapter, Belkin auto-charger, and iPod Remote switch.*

Most car stereos have a cassette player, and you can buy a cassette-player adapter from most consumer electronics stores or from the Apple Store (such as the Sony CPA-9C Car Cassette Adapter). It resembles a tape cassette with a mini-plug cable that connects through the cassette slot. You can connect the mini-plug cable directly to the iPod, or to the auto-charger if a mini-socket is offered, or to the iPod Remote switch, which in turn is connected to the iPod. Then insert the adapter into the cassette player. This is the best method for most cars because it provides the best sound quality.

Wireless Playback

A wireless music adapter lets you play music from your iPod on an FM radio with no connections or cables. You can use a wireless adapter in a car, on a boat, on the beach with a portable radio, or even in your home with a stereo system and tuner.

Connect a wireless adapter to the iPod's headphone connector or the line-out connector on the iPod's dock. A wireless adapter such as the iRock, available in the Apple Store and pictured in Figure 2.13, or the popular Belkin Tunecast Mobile FM Transmitter, acts like a miniature radio station, broadcasting to a nearby FM radio. You use a radio and tune in the appropriate frequency on the FM dial. The adapter offers a choice of several frequencies—typically 88.1, 88.3, 88.5, and 88.7 MHz. Choose a frequency, set the adapter according to its instructions, and tune your radio to the same FM frequency.

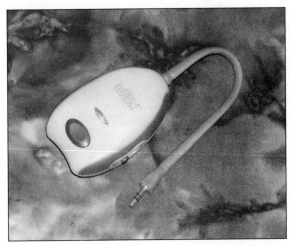

FIGURE 2.13 *The iRock wireless adapter for playing iPod music on radios tuned to the appropriate FM frequency.*

The iRock adapter, shown in Figure 2.13, uses two standard AAA alkaline batteries. You can use it with an iPod running on a battery or connected to power, but the adapter's batteries will eventually need to be replaced—the wireless adapter lacks any connection for AC power. It needs to be close enough to the radio's antenna to work, which makes it impractical for home stereos—you can get better quality sound by connecting to a home stereo with cables.

Adapting to Power

Power outlets change from country to country. If you want to charge up your iPod's battery wherever you are, you may want a travel kit of power accessories. For example, the Apple Store offers the World Travel Adapter Kit, which includes a set of six AC plugs with prongs that fit different electrical outlets around the world. The kit is designed to work with the white portable power adapter that came with your iPod. The AC plugs included in the kit support outlets in North America, Japan, China, the United Kingdom, Continental Europe, Korea, Australia, and Hong Kong.

One way to solve the power problem is to use replaceable batteries found in any convenience store. The Belkin Battery Pack, available in the Apple Store, lets you power your iPod with replaceable batteries—even when the internal battery is drained. It uses four standard AA alkaline batteries that you can replace when the charge is gone. Discreet suction cups secure the unit to the back of your iPod without marring your iPod's finish, and a charge-level indicator tells you when the batteries are running low.

Another way to provide power is to use your FireWire-equipped laptop to supply the power, and then use a power adapter with your laptop. You can use, for example, the Kensington Universal Car/Air Adapter for Apple to plug your PowerBook or iBook into any car cigarette lighter or Empower-equipped airline seat. Then use your FireWire-dock cable and dock to power your iPod (or FireWire cable alone for older iPods).

Controlling Sound Quality

If the experts on high-fidelity sound agree on one thing, it is that there is no exact scientific definition of a high-fidelity system. The limitations of the human ear and variations in human taste, room acoustics, system distortions, and ambient noise all contribute to this fundamental inconsistency of opinion.

High-fidelity stereos compensate by providing ways to improve the sound quality without changing the sound source. When you turn up the bass or treble on a stereo system, you are actually increasing the volume, or intensity, of certain frequencies while the music is playing. You are not actually changing the sound itself, just the way it is amplified and produced through speakers.

The type of equalizer (EQ) found in iTunes and MusicMatch Jukebox lets you fine-tune specific sound frequencies in a more precise way than with bass and treble controls. You might pick, for example, entirely different equalizer settings for car speakers, home speakers, and headphones, or for different genres of music.

The iPod also has a built-in equalizer, but you can't directly change individual frequencies—it offers *presets* for a variety of specific musical genres and listening environments. You can use the iPod's equalizer for "on the fly" adjustments of the sound by choosing a preset on the iPod. You can also use the iTunes or MusicMatch Jukebox equalizer to improve or enhance the sound, assigning built-in settings or your own custom equalizer settings to each song, and these settings can then be used by the iPod.

Your iPod's Equalizer

As your environment changes, so does your perception of sound. You may have terrific low (bass) and high (treble) frequencies when driving in the country or jogging in the woods, but you may wish to boost these frequencies when driving on a freeway or riding in a boat or airplane, where excess noise in the environment might drown out the sound.

The iPod's built-in equalizer modifies the volume of the frequencies of the sound, and, while you don't have sliders for making adjustments like the iTunes and MusicMatch Jukebox equalizers (described in Chapter 4), you get the same long list of presets to suit the type of music or the type of environment.

To select an iPod equalizer preset, choose Settings from the main menu, which displays the Settings menu as shown in Figure 2.14. Choose EQ from the Settings menu, and select one of the presets as shown in Figure 2.15.

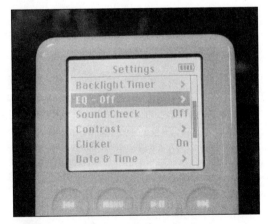

FIGURE 2.14 *Choosing EQ from the Settings menu, which appears after choosing Settings from the iPod's main menu.*

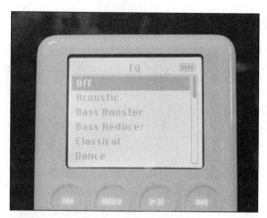

FIGURE 2.15   *Choosing an equalizer preset for the iPod's sound in the EQ menu.*

Each EQ preset offers a different balance of frequencies designed to enhance the sound in certain ways. For example, Bass Booster increases the volume of the low (bass) frequencies, while Treble Booster does the same to the high (treble) frequencies.

The Off setting turns off the iPod's equalizer—no presets are used, not even one you may have assigned in iTunes or MusicMatch Jukebox. You must choose an EQ setting to turn on your iPod's equalizer.

Custom Equalizer Settings

If you have already assigned a preset to a song using iTunes or MusicMatch Jukebox (as described in Chapter 4), your iPod uses the assigned EQ preset. The assigned EQ preset from iTunes or MusicMatch Jukebox takes precedence over any preset EQ you choose for your iPod.

If you know in advance that certain songs should have specific presets assigned to them, use iTunes or MusicMatch Jukebox to assign the preset equalization to the song before copying the song to your iPod (see Chapter 4). On the other hand, if you don't want to preordain your songs to have a certain preset and want to experiment with your iPod's presets to improve playback in different listening environments, *don't* assign a preset—wait until you have the song in your iPod, and then you can apply different EQ presets on the song.

If you assign a preset to a song in iTunes or MusicMatch Jukebox, you can use it by turning on the iPod's equalizer—choose any EQ setting (other than Off), and the iPod uses the song's preset for playback.

Setting Consistent Volume for All Songs

Music CDs are all mastered differently, with discrepancies in volume between songs on different albums (and sometimes between songs on the same album). On your iPod, you can standardize the volume of all the songs in your music library with the Sound Check feature in iTunes, or the Volume Leveling feature in MusicMatch Jukebox. You can then turn this feature on or off by choosing Sound Check from Settings in the iPod main menu.

iTunes Sound Check

In iTunes, to have all the songs in your library play at the same volume level, choose iTunes>Preferences, and click the Effects button to see the Effects preferences. Then turn on the Sound Check check box, as shown in Figure 2.16. This sets all the songs to the current volume controlled by the iTunes volume slider.

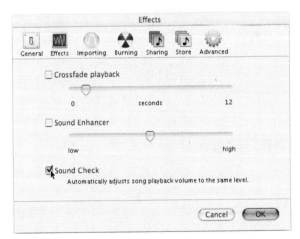

FIGURE 2.16 *Turning on the Sound Check option in the iTunes Effects preferences for the entire music library.*

MusicMatch Jukebox Volume Leveling

In MusicMatch Jukebox, follow these steps:

1. Select the songs to be processed in the library.

2. Right-click (the alternate mouse button) the selection to display the pop-up menu, and choose Prepare Tracks for Volume Leveling. Volume-leveled tracks have a green musical note icon next to them.

You can also choose to volume-level your entire library (or just selected tracks or playlists) by choosing Options>Player>Volume Leveling. Note that it may take a long time (perhaps overnight) to prepare an entire music library for volume leveling. The music itself is not changed; the software simply adds information about how to amplify the sound when the Volume Leveling feature is turned on.

Finally, to make sure your iPod receives the volume leveling information, select the iPod in the PortablesPlus window under the Attached Portable Devices folder, and click the Options button, then the Audio tab, as shown in Figure 2.17. Turn on the "Apply volume leveling" option so that music copied to your iPod includes the volume leveling information.

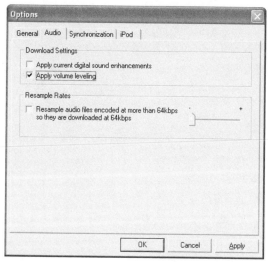

FIGURE 2.17   *Turning on the volume leveling (Sound Check) option in MusicMatch Jukebox for music copied to the iPod.*

iPod Sound Check

The iPod offers a way to turn this "sound check" (a.k.a. "volume leveling") feature on or off. To have all songs play at the same volume level all the time, choose Settings>Sound Check>On to turn on the sound check feature. To turn it off, choose Settings>Sound Check>Off.

You now have the basic skills for getting songs into your iPod (as described in Chapter 1), and playing music on your iPod, as described in this chapter. But there is a lot more you can do with the software that comes with your iPod—iTunes for the Mac, and MusicMatch Jukebox for the PC. The next chapter provides details on how to manage your music library, organize songs and song information, and update your iPod in different ways—automatically, by playlist, or manually.

Chapter 3

Managing Your
Music Library

Here's what you'll explore in this chapter:

- ◆ Getting and editing song information from the Internet
- ◆ Browsing and locating songs in the iTunes and MusicMatch Jukebox music libraries
- ◆ Updating your iPod automatically or manually, and copying songs and playlists to your iPod
- ◆ Managing music files, sharing music, and backing up your music library

Your iPod's music can be a complete copy of your music library or some portion of it. You can set up your iPod to update automatically or manually—either way, the changes you make to your library can be reflected in your iPod.

In this chapter, you'll learn how to organize your songs and browse your library to find and display songs sorted by artist, album, music genre, or other attributes. You'll also learn how to grab song information from the Internet and how to edit your song information to help you select songs in your iPod.

This chapter also explains how to create a playlist—a list of songs that can be transferred to an iPod or burned to a CD—using either iTunes or MusicMatch Jukebox. iTunes even offers "smart" playlists that generate lists based on the song information (which is another good reason to edit the information). You will also learn how to make a backup of your music library, to preserve your music (especially the songs you've purchased from online music stores).

Obtaining and Using Song Information

Organization depends on *information*. Your computer can do a lot more than store your songs with "Untitled Disc" and "Track 1" as the only identifiers. Song names, album titles, genre definitions, and composer credits may seem trivial, but you can use this information to browse songs on your iPod and to create smart playlists in iTunes.

Getting Information from the Internet

You can get information about most commercial CDs from the Internet. However, you need to check your Internet connection first.

◆ If you use an always-on broadband Internet service (e.g., DSL or cable modem), you probably want iTunes or MusicMatch Jukebox to connect and retrieve song information automatically.

◆ If you're using a dial-up modem, if your Internet service is intermittently off, or if your Internet service charges prohibit using it all the time, you probably don't want this connection to be automatic.

The Internet and iTunes

When you first start iTunes, the Setup Assistant helps you through the process of setting it up. One question you answer during this process is, "Automatically connect to the Internet, or ask first?" If you click Yes, to connect automatically, your song information is automatically supplied when you insert an audio CD. It just takes a few seconds, and the information should appear. If you click No, to ask first, iTunes asks if it can connect to the Internet whenever you insert an audio CD.

If you want to change these settings at any time, you can do the following:

1. Choose iTunes>Preferences.
2. Click the General button.
3. Turn on or off the "Connect to Internet when needed" option. When on, iTunes connects automatically; when off, iTunes asks first.

If you're not automatically connected, you can connect to the Internet manually at any time and get the song information when you need it. Once you are connected, choose Advanced>Get CD Track Names.

 TIP

Even if you are automatically connected, the song information database on the Internet could be momentarily unavailable, or you may experience a delayed response. If at first you don't succeed, try Advanced>Get CD Track Names again.

The information for iTunes comes from The Gracenote CDDB® service. (CDDB stands for CD database.) The Gracenote CDDB service offers the largest online database of music information in the world. iTunes finds the track information by first looking up a key identifying number stored on every publicly released music CD. iTunes uses this number to find the information within the database. The site for Gracenote's CDDB service (http://www.gracenote.com) lets you search for music CDs by artist, song title, and other criteria. CDDB keeps track information for most of the music CDs that are released in the global commercial market. While it doesn't contain any information about personal or custom CDs, people can submit information to the database about custom or obscure CDs that the database doesn't yet know about. To submit information from within iTunes, type the information for each track while the audio CD is in your Mac, and then choose Advanced>Submit CD Track Names. This command sends the information you typed back to the CDDB site.

The Internet and MusicMatch Jukebox

In MusicMatch Jukebox, you can enable CD Lookup to grab information from the Internet by choosing Options>Settings and clicking the CD Lookup/Connectivity tab, as shown in Figure 3.1. Turn on the "Enable CD Lookup service" option.

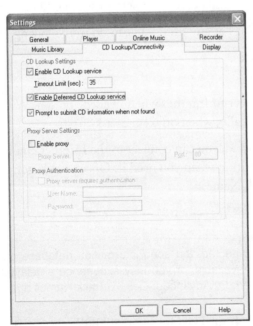

FIGURE 3.1 *Enabling CD Lookup in MusicMatch Jukebox to grab song information from the Internet.*

You can set an optional timeout limit, in seconds, for the amount of time MusicMatch Jukebox should spend trying to access the database before giving up. (Internet databases may be offline for a number of reasons, or your Internet connection may not be working.)

MusicMatch Jukebox lets you defer CD Lookup for another time, when your Internet connection is active. By default, MusicMatch Jukebox is set to enable deferred service, assuming most users are intermittently connected to the Internet. This is set by default so that you can record CDs to your music library and have MusicMatch Jukebox look up the information later, when your computer is connected to the Internet. You can change this by turning off the "Enable Deferred CD Lookup service" option.

When you record audio CDs, MusicMatch Jukebox connects to the Internet and retrieves the song information automatically, or defers this action until your computer is connected (unless you turned off these options). MusicMatch Jukebox refers to song information as "tags," and you can always edit your "tag" (song) information manually.

Editing Song Information

The song information on the Internet may not be exactly as you want it. For example, solo artists are listed with their first and last names, as in "John Lennon," but you may want to list them with their last names first, so that you can look up "Lennon, John" under "L" rather than looking up "John Lennon" under "J." You may also want to remove the word "The" from band names such as "The Who" and list the band under "Who." (In previous versions of iTunes, many bands were listed alphabetically in the "T" section under "The," but the 4.0 version of iTunes ignores "The" and sorts band names correctly.)

Editing Song Information in iTunes

In iTunes, you can edit a song's track information by clicking directly on the field and clicking again so that the pointer turns into an editing cursor, as shown in Figure 3.2. You can then select the text and type over it, or use Command-C (copy) or Command-X (cut) and Command-V (paste) to move around tiny bits of text within the field. It's just like any other text field, only smaller. As you can see in Figure 3.2, I changed the Artist field to "Beck, Jeff."

FIGURE 3.2 *Clicking inside the Artist field in iTunes to edit the information.*

You can edit the Song Name, Artist, Album, Genre, and My Ratings fields right in the song list. It may be easier, however, to edit this information with the File>Get Info command, which displays the song information window.

In most cases, if the CD's track information from CDDB is incorrect, the information is incorrect for *all* the tracks. You can edit the information for all the songs at once by following these steps:

1. Select a range or group of songs.

   To select a range of songs, click on the first song, and then hold down the Shift key while clicking on the last song, as shown in Figure 3.3. You can add to a selection by Shift-clicking other songs, and you can remove songs from the selection by holding down the Command key when clicking.

2. Choose File>Get Info, or press Command-I.

   The Get Info command displays the warning message, "Are you sure you want to edit information for multiple items?" whenever you select multiple songs. (See the following Note.)

3. Click Yes to edit information for multiple items. The Multiple Song Information window appears, as shown in Figure 3.4.

4. Edit the Artist field for the multiple songs.

>
> ### NOTE
>
> Be careful not to edit the song name when editing multiple songs at once. If you do, every song in your selection will have the same song name. I recommend leaving the warning option "Do not ask me again" unchecked, so that the warning appears whenever you edit the information for multiple songs.

When you edit a field, a check mark appears automatically in the box next to the field. The check mark indicates that the field will be changed when you click OK. Before clicking OK, make sure no other box is checked except those fields you want changed. Then click OK, and iTunes changes the fields for the entire selection of songs.

FIGURE 3.3   *Selecting a range of songs in iTunes to change the artist name for multiple songs at once.*

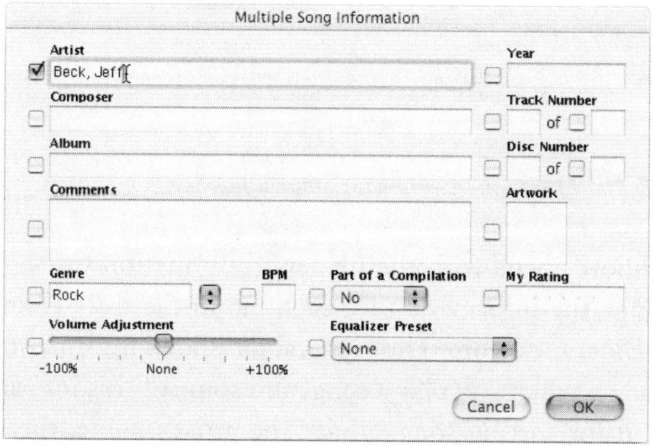

FIGURE 3.4   *Changing the artist name for multiple songs in the Multiple Song Information window in iTunes.*

TIP

In iTunes, you can edit the song information before importing the audio tracks from a CD. The edited track information for the CD is imported with the music.

Editing Song Information in MusicMatch Jukebox

The song information retrieved using the CD Lookup service can be changed after you've recorded a CD into your MusicMatch Jukebox music library. You can edit the "tag" information for a single song or for an entire album of songs at once.

To edit the information for a single song, select the song and click the Tag button (or right-click the song and choose Edit Track Tags) to open the Edit Track Tags window, as shown in Figure 3.5.

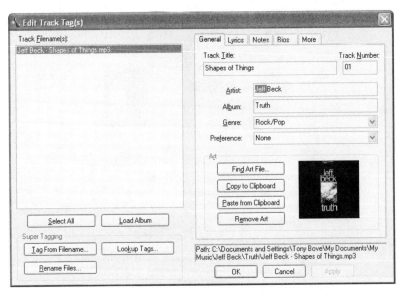

FIGURE 3.5 *Editing the song ("tag") information in MusicMatch Jukebox.*

The Edit Track Tags window opens with the General information (as shown in Figure 3.5). You can change the information for each tab in the Edit Track Tags window—Lyrics, Notes, Bios, and More. The General tab shows information that appears in the Player window when you play a song, and some of this information is transferred to your iPod for sorting songs under the artist's name, the album name, and so on.

You can edit the song information for multiple songs at once. To edit all the songs from a particular album, follow these steps:

1. Select one of the songs, and click the Tag button (or right-click the song and choose Edit Track Tags) to open the Edit Track Tags window.

2. Click the Load Album button in the lower-left side of the Edit Track Tags window.

   The Load Album button loads all the songs from the album into the list on the left side of the window, as shown in Figure 3.6.

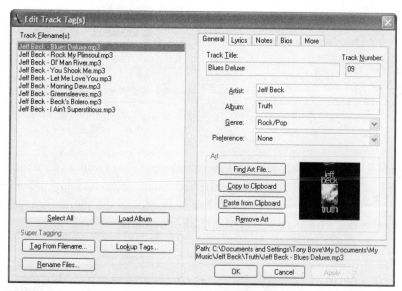

FIGURE 3.6   *Loading an album of songs to change the song ("tag") information in MusicMatch Jukebox.*

At this point you can click on each song in the album and change its information, as shown in Figure 3.5, or you can click the Select All button to select all the songs in the album and change information for all the songs at once (such as the artist's name), as shown in Figure 3.7.

When you edit a tag for multiple songs, a check mark appears automatically in the box next to the tag. The check mark indicates that the tag will be changed when you click OK or Apply. Before clicking OK or Apply, make sure no other box is checked except the tags you want changed. Then click OK, and MusicMatch Jukebox changes the tags for the entire album of songs.

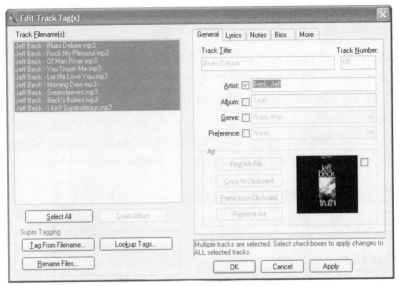

FIGURE 3.7 *Changing the artist's name for an entire album of songs in MusicMatch Jukebox.*

In the music library, MusicMatch Jukebox lists your songs under the artist name, as shown in Figure 3.8. If you change the artist name for an album of songs, the location of the music in your library changes, because the names are sorted in alphabetical order. However, the filenames do not change.

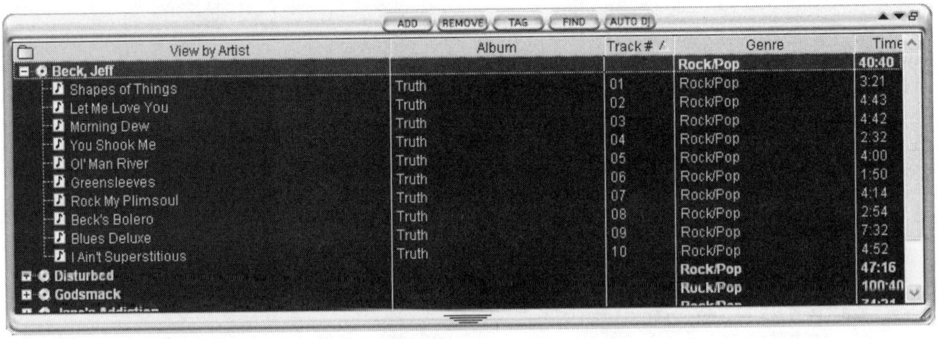

FIGURE 3.8 *After changing the artist's name for an entire album of songs, MusicMatch Jukebox reorganizes the music library to list the songs under the edited artist name.*

TIP

When you change the artist's name for an album of songs, you may also want to change the filenames stored on disk to reflect this change, so that when you start MusicMatch Jukebox again, the proper artist name can be retrieved from the filename if necessary. To do this, use the super-tagging feature: right-click the artist name, and choose Super Tagging>Rename Files. MusicMatch Jukebox displays the current name and new name for each song, and you can click OK if you want to make the change.

Adding More Information

Adding more information about songs makes it possible to use the criteria of your choice—e.g., composer name, genre, or your personal ratings—to locate songs in your music library and iPod. In many cases, composer credits are not included in the information grabbed from the Internet, but if you add them with iTunes, you can scroll music in your library or iPod by composer as well as by artist, album, and song. (MusicMatch Jukebox, as of this writing, does not offer a Composer tag.)

Adding Information in iTunes

Once your songs are imported into the music library, locate a single song and choose File>Get Info (or Command-I). You should see the Song Information window, as shown in Figure 3.9.

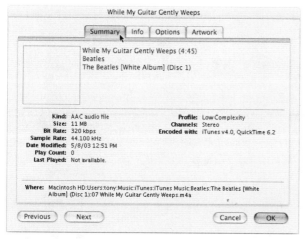

FIGURE 3.9   *Viewing and editing more song information in iTunes.*

You can change the information by clicking on each of these tabs.

◆ **Summary:** The Summary pane offers useful information about the music file's format, location on your hard disk, file size, bit rate and sample rate, and so on.

◆ **Info:** The Info pane lets you change the song name, artist, composer, album, genre, and year, and lets you add comments, as shown in Figure 3.10.

◆ **Options:** The Options pane offers volume adjustment, choice of equalizer preset, ratings, and start and stop times for each song, as shown in Figure 3.11.

◆ **Artwork:** The Artwork pane lets you add artwork for the song or delete artwork that came with the song. (The Apple Music Store supplies artwork with most songs.)

iTunes also lets you add your own ratings to songs. In the Options panel of the Song Information window, as shown in Figure 3.11, you can assign up to five stars to a song. Click to add each star, or drag across to add a set of stars at once.

You may have noticed the playlist in the left column of iTunes called "My Top Rated." This is an example of a *smart playlist*—a playlist that updates itself when ratings are changed. The "My Top Rated" playlist plays all the top-rated songs in your library. Like all other playlists, this playlist can be transferred to your iPod so that you can have the same choices.

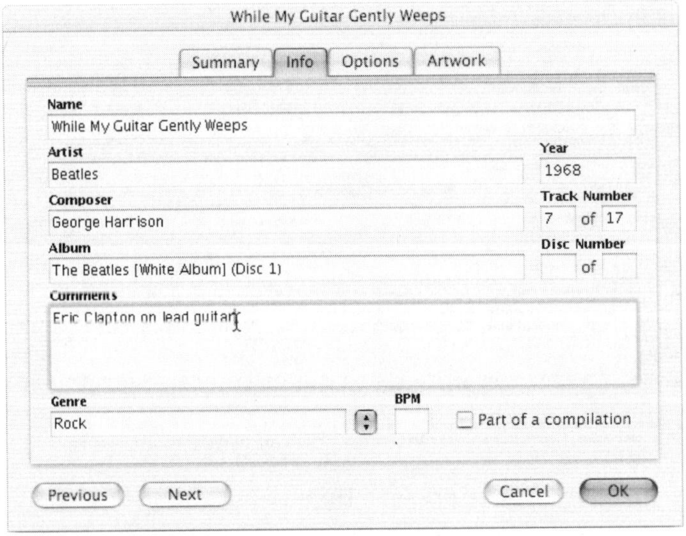

FIGURE 3.10 *Editing information in the Info pane of the Song Information window in iTunes.*

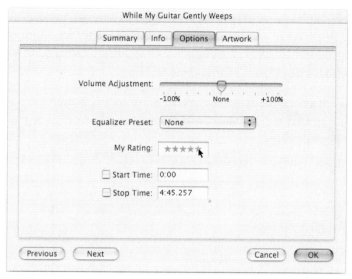

FIGURE 3.11 *Adding a rating for a song in the Options pane of the Song Information window in iTunes.*

Adding Information in MusicMatch Jukebox

Once your songs are recorded into the music library, locate a single song and click the Tag button (or right-click the song and choose Edit Track Tags). You should see the Edit Track Tags window, which provides a list of songs for an album (if you click Load Album), and shows the hard disk path to the file for the selected songs. You can change the information by clicking on each of these tabs:

◆ **General:** This tab shows the track title, artist name, album title, genre, and preference. It also offers album artwork retrieved from the song information database on the Internet—or you can add your own artwork.

◆ **Lyrics:** This tab lets you add the lyrics to songs. You can copy the lyrics from a text editor (such as Notepad or Microsoft Word) and paste them into the empty text box.

◆ **Notes:** This tab lets you add notes and comments, as shown in Figure 3.12. You can copy information from a text editor and paste it into the empty text box.

◆ **Bios:** This tab lets you add musician credits or other information (such as liner notes) to songs. You can copy this information from a text editor and paste it into the empty text box.

◆ **More:** This tab lets you categorize your songs by tempo, mood, and situation, specify the year of release, and add URLs (Internet addresses) for more information, as shown in Figure 3.13. You can also specify whether the song should be prepared for volume leveling.

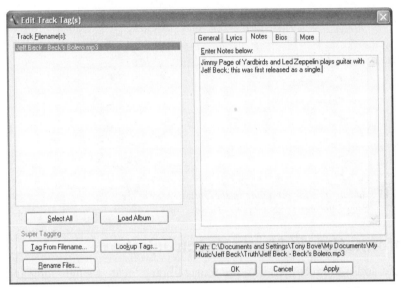

FIGURE 3.12 *Adding notes to the song information in MusicMatch Jukebox.*

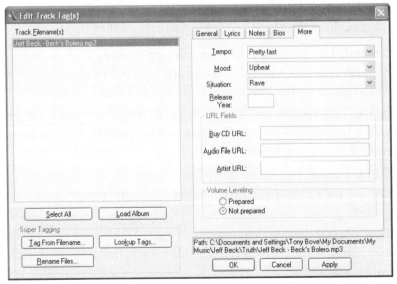

FIGURE 3.13 *Adding more information ("tags") to a song in MusicMatch Jukebox.*

Although most of this added information is not transferred to the iPod (only the information in the General tab is transferred), the information makes it easier to find music in the library and prepare playlists for different occasions. You can, for example, select all of your up-tempo songs for a playlist, and transfer that playlist to your iPod for listening on an upbeat day.

Finding and Displaying Songs

When you update your iPod automatically, all the songs in your library are transferred to your iPod. However, if you want to update your iPod manually with specific songs or albums, you need to be able to find these songs and albums in the library quickly. Using either iTunes or MusicMatch Jukebox, you can sort the list of songs and locate songs or albums. You can then drag them to playlists or directly to your iPod, as described later in this chapter.

Browsing Songs

Songs are first listed in the library in track order within albums, and albums are listed under the artist's name. This organization reflects the way the music files are stored on disk. iTunes and MusicMatch Jukebox have different interfaces and styles for organizing their music libraries, but the functions are basically the same.

Browsing Songs in iTunes

When you first use iTunes, the song list displays a long list of songs in your library, and you can scroll the list to find songs. You can also browse the library by artist and album.

To select Browse view, click the Browse icon in the upper-right corner, as shown in Figure 3.14. iTunes organizes your music library by Artist and Album by default, making it easier to find songs. Click on the Browse button again to switch out of Browse view.

The Browse view displays the songs in a list underneath a set of columns. When you click an artist in the Artist column on the left side, as shown in Figure 3.15, the album titles appear in the Albums column on the right. At the top of this Albums column, the selection "All" is highlighted, and all of the Artists' songs appear in the Song Names list below the columns.

FIGURE 3.14 *Clicking Browse to peruse the iTunes Library.*

FIGURE 3.15 *Selecting an Artist in Browse view in iTunes to see
the list of Albums for that artist.*

You can select any artist and see that artist's albums and songs. Scroll down the
Artist column and click on, for example, Hot Tuna, and iTunes displays only the
Hot Tuna albums in your collection. Each album is listed in the Album column.
What if you'd like to see everything by both Hot Tuna and Jefferson Airplane?
After clicking on Hot Tuna, scroll down the Artist column, then hold down the
Command key and click on Jefferson Airplane. iTunes displays all of the albums
and songs by both bands. As you click on different albums in the Albums column,
the Song Names list displays the songs from that album in proper track order.

Browsing Songs in MusicMatch Jukebox

When you first open MusicMatch Jukebox, the music library window displays songs in a similar fashion as Windows Explorer, with songs appearing as files within a folder that uses the artist's name, as shown in Figure 3.16 (showing the songs from the album *All That You Can't Leave Behind*, by the artist U2). Clicking the plus sign next to an artist's name opens the artist as if it were a folder; clicking the minus sign closes the "folder."

FIGURE 3.16 *Browsing the songs by U2 in MusicMatch Jukebox.*

You can change your music library's display of songs to view by album, artist, genre, or even album art. To change the viewing of songs for browsing, click the folder icon in the View By column, as shown in Figure 3.17, which displays a pop-up menu for choosing different ways to view the songs, as shown in Figure 3.18.

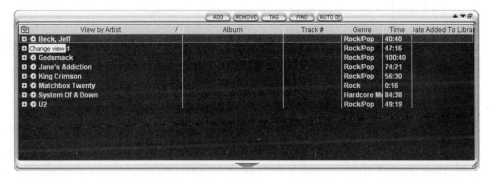

FIGURE 3.17 *Clicking the folder icon in the View By column in MusicMatch Jukebox to change the column's viewing options.*

FIGURE 3.18 *Selecting a different way to view the song list in MusicMatch Jukebox.*

When you select to view by album cover art, as shown in Figure 3.19, the album covers appear in the music library, with pop-up text balloons appearing over each album (see Figure 3.20) as you move your mouse over them, showing the song list.

 TIP

If you double-click a song in the list, or double-click an album, the song or songs appear in the playlist window and start playing. You can clear the playlist by clicking the Clear button under the playlist.

Viewing and Sorting Options

Both iTunes and MusicMatch Jukebox let you customize the music library's display to show more or less information, or different information, in the columns. With either program, you can specify what columns to show and in what order to show them, and you can make columns wider or narrower. You can also sort the listing by the column headings.

FIGURE 3.19 *Changing the view of the song list in MusicMatch Jukebox to view by album cover.*

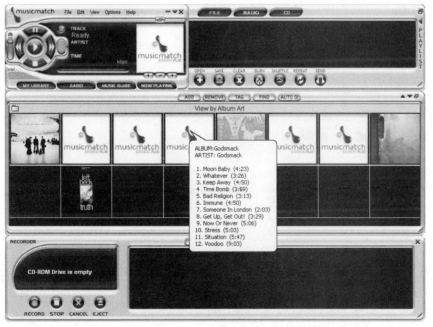

FIGURE 3.20 *Viewing the song list by album cover in MusicMatch Jukebox.*

Viewing and Sorting in iTunes

To make a column wider or narrower in iTunes, drag the dividing line between the column and the next column. As you move your cursor over the divider, it changes to a double-ended arrow, and you can click and drag the divider to change the column's width. You can also change the order of columns from left to right by clicking on a column header and dragging the entire column to the left or right.

You can add or remove columns such as Size (for file size), Date and Year (for the date the album was released, or any other date you choose for each song), Bit Rate, Sample Rate, Track Number, and Comment.

To make changes to the viewing options, choose Edit>View Options. The View Options window appears, as shown in Figure 3.21, and you can select the columns to show. To pick a column that you want to appear on the list, click the check box next to the column header so that a check mark appears. An unchecked column header indicates a column that will not appear. Note that the Song Names column will always appear in the listing and can't be removed.

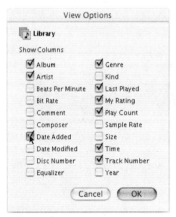

FIGURE 3.21 *Viewing options in iTunes for the song list.*

 TIP

iTunes also lets you browse by genre. To add a Genre column to the browser, choose Preferences from the iTunes menu, click the General button at the top of the preferences window, and click the box next to "Show genre when browsing."

Whether you are in Browse view or normal view, the column headers also act as sorting options. For example, if you click on the Time header above the Time column in the listing, as shown in Figure 3.22, the songs are reordered by their duration in ascending order—starting with the shortest song. If you click the Time header again, the sort is reversed, starting with the longest song.

FIGURE 3.22   *Sorting the iTunes song list by the Time column, with the shortest song first.*

The arrow indicator in the header indicates whether the sort is in ascending or descending order. When the arrow is pointing up, the sort is in ascending order; when down, it is in descending order.

You can also sort the song list in alphabetical order. Click on the Artist header to sort all the songs in the list by the artist name, in alphabetical order, starting with the letter "A" (the arrow points up). Click it again to sort the list in reverse alphabetical order, starting with "Z" (the arrow points down).

Viewing and Sorting in MusicMatch Jukebox

To make a column wider or narrower in MusicMatch Jukebox, drag the dividing line between the column and the next column.

To change the columns in the song list, choose Options>Settings>Music Library to display the Settings window, as shown in Figure 3.23 (or choose Options>Settings and click the Music Library tab). In the "View by" pop-up menu, you can change the first column of the song listing, which typically is the column used for sorting the list.

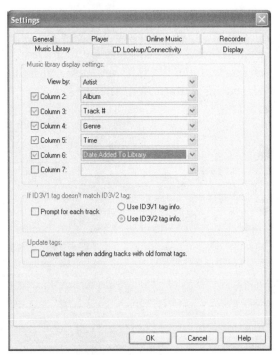

FIGURE 3.23   *Changing the music library display settings in MusicMatch Jukebox to add a column to the song list.*

You can choose up to six more columns (for a total of seven) to display in the song list. To pick the type of information for a column, click the check box for the column so that a check mark appears, and choose the type of information ("tag") for that column. An unchecked column header indicates a column that will not appear. For example, in Figure 3.23, column 6 is defined to show the "Date Added to Library" information, which appears as the far-right column (the sixth column) in the song list, as shown in Figure 3.24.

 TIP

You can also right-click any column heading in the MusicMatch Jukebox song list to change the type of information it shows.

The column headers also act as sorting options—click once to sort in ascending order, and click again to sort in descending order. The arrow indicator in the header indicates whether the sort is in ascending or descending order—when the arrow is pointing up, the sort is in ascending order; when down, it is in descending order.

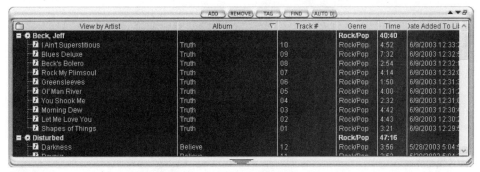

FIGURE 3.24 *The song list in MusicMatch Jukebox now shows a sixth column with "Date Added to Library."*

Searching for Songs

Sometimes you just want to find a specific song, or a set of songs that have the same word in their names (such as all songs whose titles include the word "love") or the same spelling of an artist's name. Both iTunes and MusicMatch Jukebox provide the ability to search for songs.

Searching for Songs in iTunes

In iTunes, you can search for songs using the Search field, which is the oval field in the top-right corner, to the left of the Browse button, as shown in Figure 3.25. Click inside this field, and type the first characters of the song title, or the artist, or the album title. The search operation works immediately, searching for matches in the Song Name, Artist, and Album columns of the listing, and displaying matches as you type.

Typing very few characters results in a long list of possible songs, but the search narrows down as you type additional characters. iTunes searches all the columns of the song information including Genre, Composer, and so on. The search results include songs with the characters in the title or artist name, and there is no distinction between upper- and lowercase characters.

If you want to search the entire library, first click the "All" selection at the top of the Artist column, so that you are browsing the entire library, before using the Search field. Or, if you prefer, turn off the Browse view by clicking the Browse button again, and use the Search field with the library's song list.

To back out of a search so that the full list appears again, you can either click the circled X in the Search field, or delete the characters in the Search field. You should then see the entire list of songs in your library, just as it was before.

FIGURE 3.25 *Type a few characters in the iTunes Search field to locate songs and artist names that match.*

Searching for Songs in MusicMatch Jukebox

To search for a song in MusicMatch Jukebox, click the Find button in the music library window to display the Find in Music Library window, as shown in Figure 3.26. Type part or all of a song name's characters, and click Find First (or OK).

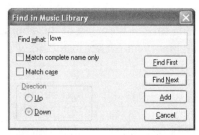

FIGURE 3.26 *Find songs in the MusicMatch Jukebox music library by typing a few characters that match with song names.*

MusicMatch Jukebox lists the first match for the characters in the Find window. You can continue to find more matches by clicking Find Next. Clicking Add adds the song to your current playlist. (Playlists are the next topic in this chapter.)

You can use the "Match complete name only" and "Match case" options to refine your search. To match the complete name, you must type the entire song name. To match case, you must type the name exactly as it appears in the list, with upper- and lowercase characters.

Using Playlists

You can always create a temporary "On-The-Go Playlist" while you are on the go with your iPod, as described in Chapter 2. However, one big advantage of the iPod–computer connection is the ability to define playlists for your library that you can also use in your iPod.

Playlists are essentially lists of songs. You would typically create a playlist in order to burn a CD—arranging the songs in the playlist as you wish, to appear in that order on the CD. You can also use playlists to organize your music and play DJ. You might want to create playlists specifically for use with an iPod on road trips, and others that combine songs from different albums based on themes or similarities.

You can create as many playlists of songs, in any order, as you want. The music files don't change, nor are they copied—only their names are stored in the playlists. In iTunes, you can even create a "smart playlist" that can automatically add songs to itself based on the criteria you set up.

Creating a Playlist

In either iTunes or MusicMatch Jukebox, you can drag individual songs or entire albums into a playlist and rearrange the songs quickly and easily. You can then use playlists to organize your music and, if you wish, use playlists to update your iPod rather than updating with your entire music library (as described later in this chapter).

Creating a Playlist in iTunes

To create a playlist in iTunes, click the + button in the bottom-left corner of the iTunes window, or choose File>New Playlist. The playlist appears in the Source list, as shown in Figure 3.27. After you give it a new name, iTunes automatically sorts it into alphabetical order in the Source list, underneath the preset smart playlists and other sources.

To add songs to your playlist, select the entire music library by clicking Library in the Source list. You can then drag songs from the song list over the name of the playlist to add the songs. You can also turn on Browse mode to find songs easier, as shown in Figure 3.28.

FIGURE 3.27 *Creating and naming a new playlist in the Source list in iTunes.*

FIGURE 3.28 *Adding songs to the new playlist in iTunes.*

The order of songs in the playlist is based on the order in which you dragged them to the list. You can rearrange the list by dragging songs within the playlist, as shown in Figure 3.29. To drag a song up the list and scroll at the same time, drag it over the up arrow in the first column (the song number); to drag it down the list and scroll, drag it to the bottom of the list. You can drag a group of songs at once by selecting them (using click and Shift-click or Command-click).

FIGURE 3.29   *Dragging a song to a new position within the playlist in iTunes.*

You can drag songs into a playlist from any other playlist. Remember, only links are copied, not the actual files. You can also select multiple songs at once and drag the bunch over a playlist. Besides dragging songs, you can also rearrange a playlist by sorting the list—by clicking on the column headings Song Name, Time, Artist, and so on. And when you double-click a playlist, it opens in its own window, displaying the song list.

 TIP

To create a playlist quickly, select multiple songs at once (using Shift-click or Command-click), and then choose File>New Playlist From Selection. You can then type a name for your new playlist.

You might want to play entire albums of songs without having to select each album. To create a playlist of entire albums in a particular order, follow these steps:

1. Create a playlist by clicking the + sign under the Source list, or choosing File>New Playlist. Type a name for your new playlist.

2. Click the Library in the Source list, and click Browse to find the artist. The Album list appears in the right panel, as shown in Figure 3.30.

3. Drag the album name over the playlist name.

4. Drag each subsequent album over the playlist name.

FIGURE 3.30 *Dragging an entire album in iTunes to a playlist, preserving the album's track order.*

This is the easiest way to drag an entire album into a playlist and maintain its track sequence. Each time you drag an album, iTunes automatically lists the songs in the proper track sequence.

Creating a Playlist in MusicMatch Jukebox

To create a playlist in MusicMatch Jukebox, you can either double-click each song you want to add to a playlist or drag a selection of songs to the playlist window. With either method, the songs appear in a list in the Playlist window, as shown in Figure 3.31. To select a range of songs, click on the first song, and then hold down the Shift key while clicking on the last song. To add single songs to your selection, hold down the Control key while clicking on them.

FIGURE 3.31 *After selecting songs in the MusicMatch Jukebox music library, you can drag them to the playlist window.*

To save the songs in the playlist window with a playlist name (essential for transferring playlists to the iPod), click the Save button, and give the playlist a name, as shown in Figure 3.32.

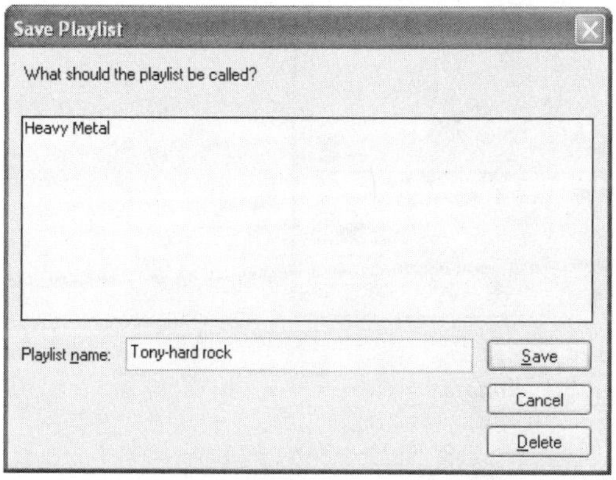

FIGURE 3.32 *After clicking the Save button in the MusicMatch Jukebox playlist window, give your playlist a name.*

After saving a playlist, click the Clear button to clear the playlist window, so that you can load a new set of songs to create another playlist.

You might want to play entire albums of songs without having to select each one. To create a playlist of entire albums in a particular order, follow these steps:

1. Select one or more albums in the music library.
2. Drag the album or albums into the playlist window.
3. Save your playlist by clicking the Save button, and type a name for your new playlist.
4. Click the Clear button to clear the playlist.

To open a saved playlist, click the Open (+) button in the playlist window, and click the Playlists icon in the left column of the Open Music window, as shown in Figure 3.33. You can then select any named playlist, and MusicMatch Jukebox loads the playlist into the playlist window for playback.

You can leave on the option to "Clear current playlist when adding new tracks" so that you replace the current tracks in the playlist window with the new playlist.

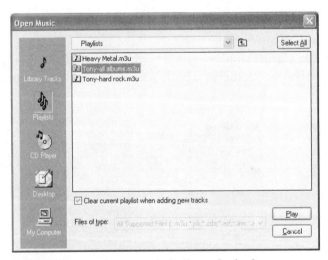

FIGURE 3.33 *Opening a saved playlist to play in the MusicMatch Jukebox playlist window.*

Using Smart Playlists (iTunes Only)

The playlists at the top of the Source list, indicated by a gear icon, are "smart" playlists supplied with iTunes—they add songs to themselves based on prearranged criteria. For example, My Top Rated is a smart playlist that adds songs to its list based on your ratings.

To view and edit a smart playlist, select the playlist and choose File>Edit Smart Playlist. The Smart Playlist window appears, showing the criteria for the smart playlist, as shown in Figure 3.34. You may want to modify the smart playlist so that it picks songs with a higher rating—simply add another star or two to the My Rating criteria. You can also choose to limit the playlist to a certain number of songs, selected by various methods such as random, most recently played, and so on.

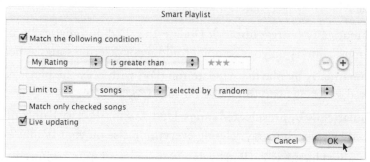

FIGURE 3.34 *Viewing and editing the criteria for the My Top Rated smart playlist in iTunes.*

To create a new smart playlist, choose File>New Smart Playlist. The Smart Playlist window appears so that you can set up your own criteria. Here's a summary of your criteria choices:

◆ **Match the following condition:** You can select from the first pop-up menu any of the categories used for song information, and select an operator such as "is greater than" or "is less than" from the second pop-up. You can also add multiple conditions by clicking the + button, and then decide whether to match all or any of these conditions.

◆ **Limit to:** You can make the smart playlist a specific duration, measured by the number of songs, or time, or size in megabytes or gigabytes. The songs can be selected by various methods such as random, most recently played, and so on.

◆ **Match only checked songs:** This selects only songs that have a black check mark beside them, along with the rest of the criteria.

◆ **Live updating:** This allows iTunes to automatically update the playlist continually, as you add or remove songs from the library.

After setting up the criteria, click OK to create your new smart playlist. iTunes creates it with a gear icon and the name "untitled playlist." Select the name and type a new name for it.

iPod Updating Options

You can set up your iPod to be updated with music in different ways, using either iTunes on the Mac or MusicMatch Jukebox on the PC.

◆ **Automatically (entire library):** Update the iPod automatically to match your music library on your computer, adding or deleting songs as necessary.

◆ **Automatically by playlist:** Update the iPod with only the playlists you've selected, deleting everything else on your iPod.

◆ **Automatically by preselected songs:** Update your iPod with only the songs marked by a check mark, deleting everything else on your iPod.

◆ **Manually:** Update your iPod by dragging songs, albums, and/or playlists to the iPod, without deleting anything. You can also manually delete songs, albums, and playlists from your iPod and edit playlists and song information directly on the iPod with this method.

Updating from the Library Automatically

Adding music to your iPod, and deleting music from your iPod, can be totally automatic. By default, the iPod is set up to update itself automatically, synchronizing itself with your music library, as described in Chapter 1.

With automatic update your iPod matches your library exactly, song for song, playlist for playlist. iTunes or MusicMatch Jukebox automatically copies everything in your music library to your iPod. If you made changes in your music library after the last time you updated your iPod, those changes are automatically made in your iPod when you connect it to the computer again. If you added or deleted songs in your library, those songs are added or deleted in your iPod's library (unless you use the "ignore all content deletions" option in MusicMatch Jukebox).

Updating from the iTunes Library

iTunes is already set up to automatically update your iPod—unless you turned off the "automatic update" option in the Setup Assistant (see below how to turn it back on). Simply connect your iPod to your Mac, and the first thing iTunes does is automatically update your iPod.

 NOTE

You can prevent your iPod from automatically updating by holding down the Command and Option keys as you connect the iPod, and keeping them held down until the iPod name appears in the iTunes Source list.

When the updating is finished, the iTunes status view says "iPod update is Complete." You can then click the iPod Eject button, which appears in the bottom-right side of the iTunes window, replacing the CD Eject button. You can also "eject" (same as "un-mount") the iPod by dragging the iPod's icon on the Finder's desktop to the trashcan. After you drag it to the trashcan, the iPod display says that it is "OK to disconnect." You can then disconnect your iPod from its dock, or disconnect the dock from the computer.

If you changed your iPod options to update manually or automatically by playlist, you can change it back to automatic update by following these steps:

1. Connect your iPod to your Mac.
2. Select the iPod in the iTunes Source list (Your iPod's name appears near the top.)
3. Click the iPod Options button (on the bottom-right side of the iTunes window, to the left of the Equalizer button, as shown in Figure 3.35) to open the iPod Preferences window.
4. Turn on the "Automatically update all songs and playlists" option in the iPod Preferences window, as shown in Figure 3.36.

After turning on this option, iTunes displays the message "Are you sure you want to enable automatic updating? All existing songs and playlists on the iPod will be replaced with songs and playlists from the iTunes music library." Click OK to go ahead. When the update is complete, click the iPod Eject button, or drag the iPod's icon on the Finder desktop to the trash.

FIGURE 3.35   *Clicking on the iPod Options button on the bottom-right side of the iTunes window to open the iPod Preferences window.*

FIGURE 3.36   *Setting up iTunes to automatically update all songs and playlists in the music library to the iPod.*

TIP

If you take your iPod to another Mac and connect it, you may be in for a surprise. When you connect an iPod that was linked to another Mac, iTunes displays the message, "This iPod is linked to another iTunes music library. Do you want to change the link to this iTunes music library and replace all existing songs and playlists on this iPod with those from this library?" If you don't want to change your iPod to have this other music library, click the No button. Otherwise, as the message says, the contents of your iPod are erased and iTunes starts to update your iPod with its library.

You may want to update your iPod automatically but only with the songs selected in your iTunes library using the check mark. To use this method you must first make the song selections by adding a check mark to songs you want to transfer to your iPod and removing the check mark from songs you don't want to transfer.

 TIP

You can quickly turn on or off the check marks for an entire album in iTunes by selecting an album in Browse view and holding down the Command key when clicking a check mark.

After marking the songs to transfer with the check mark, follow the above steps to connect your iPod and click the Options button. Turn on the "Automatically update all songs and playlists" option and click OK for the "Are you sure..." message. Then turn on the "Only update checked songs" option. iTunes automatically updates your iPod by erasing its contents and copying only the songs in the iTunes library that have a check mark.

Updating from the MusicMatch Jukebox Library

By default, MusicMatch Jukebox is set up to automatically update your iPod—unless you turned off the "Complete library synchronization" option in the Options window (see below how to turn it back on). Connect your iPod to the PC, and if MusicMatch Jukebox does not launch by itself, start the program.

Wait a few minutes for your iPod to be recognized by MusicMatch Jukebox. Your iPod should appear in the PortablesPlus window under the Attached Portable Devices folder. If the window is not yet open, choose File>Send to Portable Device to open it. When your iPod appears, select it and click the Sync button to update your iPod with the MusicMatch Jukebox music library. The PortablesPlus window displays a warning message—click Yes to continue.

When the synchronization is completed, click the Eject button at the bottom-left side of the PortablesPlus window to eject the iPod.

 NOTE

During updating, the iPod displays the warning: "Do not disconnect." Wait for the update to finish, and for the iPod to display the message, "OK to disconnect" before disconnecting it from your computer. In Windows, depending on the type of FireWire or USB connection, you may need to use the iPod for Windows Manager program (choose it from the iPod menu in your Program menu) to "unmount" the iPod.

If you changed your iPod options to update manually or automatically by playlist, you can change it back to automatic update by following these steps:

1. Connect your iPod to your PC, and wait for it to be recognized by MusicMatch Jukebox. Your iPod should appear in the PortablesPlus window under the Attached Portable Devices folder. If the window is not yet open, choose File>Send to Portable Device.

2. Select the iPod, and click the Options button, then the Synchronization tab, and choose the Complete Library synchronization option, as shown in Figure 3.37. You can also turn on the options to "Automatically synchronize on device connection" and "Ignore all content deletions."

3. Click the Sync button to update your iPod with the MusicMatch Jukebox music library. The PortablesPlus window displays a warning message—click Yes to continue.

4. When the synchronization is completed, click the Eject button at the bottom-left side of the PortablesPlus window to eject the iPod.

The Options window offers two options for automatic updating: you can set your iPod to automatically synchronize on device connection, so that each time you connect the iPod the synchronization starts immediately; and you can set it to ignore all content deletions, so that the update does not delete anything in your iPod—it simply adds more music, leaving the music on your iPod intact.

FIGURE 3.37   *Setting your iPod to automatic update (a.k.a. library synchronization) in MusicMatch Jukebox.*

 NOTE

If you turn on the option to "Automatically synchronize on device connection," your iPod will update automatically when you connect it. However, if you don't want this to happen every time, go to the Options window to turn it off. (If you just connected, you have to wait for an update to happen before you can do this.) The alternative is to leave this option off and use the Sync button when you want to update your iPod.

Updating by Playlist Automatically

If you have several iPods or music devices, or several people sharing one music library or one iPod, you may want to set up automatic updating by playlist, so that you can determine which playlists (and associated music files) are copied to the iPod automatically. Before using this update option, create the playlists that you want to copy to the iPod. If you want to copy playlists or music manually, see the next section on manual updating.

Updating by Playlist in iTunes

iTunes lets you define playlists to use to automatically update the iPod. When you use this feature, the playlists replace whatever music was on your iPod. This is for convenience, so that you can automatically switch your iPod's contents from one set of music to another, without having to use multiple music libraries.

To define playlists for automatic update:

1. Connect the iPod to your Mac.
2. Select the iPod in the iTunes Source list. The iPod's name appears near the top.
3. Click the iPod options button on the bottom-right side of the iTunes window, to the left of the Equalizer button.
4. Turn on the "Automatically update selected playlists only" option.
5. Add a check mark in the box next to each playlist to define playlists for updating, as shown in Figure 3.38. Mark all the playlists you want to copy in the update, and click OK.

iTunes automatically updates the iPod by erasing its contents and copying only the playlists you selected in step 5.

When the update is complete, click the iPod Eject button, or drag the iPod's icon on the Finder desktop to the trash.

FIGURE 3.38 *Setting up the iPod in iTunes to automatically update with only the selected playlists.*

Updating by Playlist in MusicMatch Jukebox

MusicMatch Jukebox lets you save playlists and synchronize them with an iPod automatic update. When you use this feature, you can make changes to the defined playlists in the library and the changes are automatically updated to the iPod's versions of the same playlists. You can create new playlists, define them for synchronization, and the automatic update copies the new playlists and music to the iPod.

To define playlists for automatic update:

1. Connect your iPod to your PC, and wait for it to be recognized by MusicMatch Jukebox. Your iPod should appear in the PortablesPlus window under the Attached Portable Devices folder. If the window is not yet open, choose File>Send to Portable Device.

2. Select the iPod, and click the Options button, then the Synchronization tab, and choose the "Selected playlist synchronization" option, as shown in Figure 3.39. You can also turn on the options to "Automatically synchronize on device connection" and "Ignore all content deletions".

3. Add a check mark in the box next to each playlist to define playlists for synchronization, as shown in Figure 3.39.

4. Click the Sync button to update your iPod with the defined playlists. The PortablesPlus window displays a warning message—click Yes to continue.

5. When the synchronization is completed, click the Eject button at the bottom left side of the PortablesPlus window to eject the iPod.

FIGURE 3.39 *Setting the iPod to update (a.k.a. synchronize) playlists in MusicMatch Jukebox.*

In the iPod, playlists appear directly under the iPod's name on the left side of the PortablesPlus window, as shown in Figure 3.40. The contents of the iPod (or the contents of the selected playlist in the iPod) appear in the right side of the window.

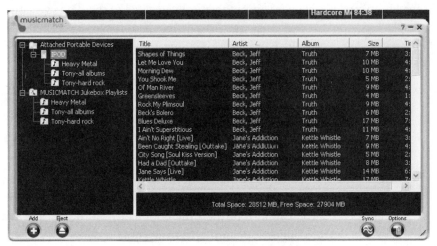

FIGURE 3.40 *Viewing the iPod's playlists in MusicMatch Jukebox.*

Updating Manually and Copying Directly

You can copy music directly to your iPod without automatic updating and synchronization. You may have one or more reasons for doing this, but here are some obvious ones:

◆ Your music library may be too big for your iPod, and, therefore, you want to copy individual albums, songs, or playlists to your iPod.

◆ You want to share a single music library with several iPods, and you have different albums that you want to copy to each iPod.

◆ You want to copy some music from another computer's music library, without deleting any music from your iPod.

You can add or delete music from your iPod using either iTunes or MusicMatch Jukebox.

Updating Manually in iTunes

When you connect the iPod to a Mac, the iPod's name appears in the iTunes Source list, and you can open it just like a folder in the Finder, displaying the iPod's playlists.

TIP

You can prevent the iPod from automatically updating when you connect it to a computer by holding down the Command and Option keys as you connect the iPod and keeping them held down until the iPod name appears in the iTunes Source list.

To copy music to your iPod directly using manual updating, follow these steps:

1. Connect your iPod to your Mac. To stop automatic updating, hold down the Command and Option keys as you connect the iPod until the iPod's name appears in the Source list.

2. Select the iPod in the iTunes Source list. Your iPod's name appears in the iTunes Source list near the top.

3. Click the iPod Options button on the bottom-right side of the iTunes window, to the left of the Equalizer button.

4. Turn on the "Manually manage songs and playlists" option, as shown in Figure 3.41.

5. After turning on this option, iTunes displays the message "Disabling automatic update requires manually unmounting the iPod before each disconnect." This means that you must drag the iPod's icon on the Finder's desktop to the trash when you finish updating. Click OK.

FIGURE 3.41 *Using the iPod options in iTunes to manage the copying of music manually.*

You can now copy albums, songs, or playlists by dragging them directly from your music library over the name of the iPod in the Source list, as shown in Figure 3.42. When you copy a playlist, all the songs associated with the playlist are copied along with the playlist itself.

FIGURE 3.42 *Copying an album of songs directly from the iTunes Library to the iPod.*

When the update is complete, click the iPod Eject button, or drag the iPod's icon on the Finder desktop to the trash.

WARNING

During updating, the iPod displays a warning: "Do not disconnect." Don't disconnect until the iPod displays the "OK to disconnect" message, or you may have to restore your iPod from scratch because of disk errors.

Updating Manually in MusicMatch Jukebox

In MusicMatch Jukebox, you can drag songs and albums directly to the iPod. The iPod's playlists appear directly under the iPod's name on the left side of the PortablesPlus window, as shown in Figure 3.43. The contents of the iPod (or the contents of the selected playlist in the iPod) appear in the right side of the window.

To copy music directly to your iPod:

1. Connect your iPod to your PC, and wait for it to be recognized by MusicMatch Jukebox. Your iPod should appear in the PortablesPlus window under the Attached Portable Devices folder. If the window is not yet open, choose File>Send to Portable Device.

2. Select the iPod so that its contents appear in the right side of the window, as shown in Figure 3.43.

3. Drag entire albums or songs from the music library window to the PortablesPlus window.

4. When the copying is completed, drag more albums or songs, or click the Eject button at the bottom-left side of the PortablesPlus window to eject the iPod.

FIGURE 3.43 *Copying an album directly to the iPod using MusicMatch Jukebox.*

WARNING

During updating, the iPod displays the warning: "Do not disconnect." Don't disconnect until the iPod displays the "OK to disconnect" message, or you may have to restore your iPod from scratch because of disk errors.

Deleting Music from Your iPod

If you update your iPod automatically, song deletion is also automatic. If you delete a song or album from your music library, the next time you update the iPod, the song or album is deleted automatically (unless you turn on the "ignore all content deletions" option in MusicMatch Jukebox). If you delete a playlist from your library, the playlist on your iPod is deleted automatically.

However, if you are manually updating your iPod, you also have to manually delete songs that you no longer want on your iPod.

Deleting Music in iTunes

The iPod's name appears in the iTunes Source list near the top. After setting the iPod to update manually, the iPod name can be opened like any other iTunes source in the list, as shown in Figure 3.44. Click the triangle next to the name to open it.

FIGURE 3.44 *Opening the iPod in the iTunes Source list.*

To delete any song in the song list, select the song and press the Delete key, or choose Edit>Clear. iTunes displays a warning to make sure you want to do this, and you can click OK to go ahead, or Cancel. You can't delete songs from a smart playlist—the Clear option is not available.

You can click the Browse button to browse the iPod's song list, just like your iTunes Library. If you want to delete an entire album, select the album and press the Delete key or choose Edit>Clear. As in the iTunes Library, if you delete a playlist, the songs themselves are not deleted.

Deleting Music in MusicMatch Jukebox

In MusicMatch Jukebox, you can delete songs directly on the iPod. The iPod's playlists appear directly under the iPod's name on the left side of the PortablesPlus window (see Figure 3.40). The contents of the iPod (or the contents of the selected playlist in the iPod) appear in the right side of the window.

To delete songs on the iPod:

1. Connect your iPod to your PC, and wait for it to be recognized by MusicMatch Jukebox. Your iPod should appear in the PortablesPlus window under the Attached Portable Devices folder. If the window is not yet open, choose File>Send to Portable Device.

2. Select the iPod so that its contents appear in the right side of the window, as shown in Figure 3.45.

3. Select one or more songs and use the alternate mouse button (right-click) to show the pop-up menu, and choose Remove.

4. When finished deleting songs, click the Eject button at the bottom-left side of the PortablesPlus window to eject the iPod.

Editing Playlists and Song Information on Your iPod

If you update your iPod automatically, any edits you make in your iTunes Library are transferred automatically. If you edit the information for a song in your music library, the next time you update the iPod, the song's editing changes are copied automatically, and if you change the order of a playlist in your library, the playlist on the iPod is changed automatically.

FIGURE 3.45 *Removing songs from the iPod using MusicMatch Jukebox.*

If you do manual updating, you have the option to edit song information and playlists in either place—in your music library, or in the iPod.

Editing in iTunes

The iPod's name appears in the iTunes Source list. After setting the iPod to update manually, the name can be opened like any other iTunes source in the list. Click the triangle next to the name to open it.

You can create as many playlists as you want, with songs in any order. The music files are not copied or moved—only their names are used in the playlists. You can even create a "smart playlist" that can automatically add songs to itself based on the criteria you set up. These playlists can be created in your iTunes music library and copied to the iPod.

You can also create playlists just on the iPod itself, in the same way:

1. Select the iPod in the iTunes Source list. The iPod's name appears in the iTunes Source list near the top.

2. Click on the + button, or choose File>New Playlist. The + button in the bottom-left corner of the iTunes window creates a new playlist.

3. The new playlist appears in the Source list under the iPod. Type a new name for it. After you change its name, iTunes automatically sorts it into alphabetical order in the list under the iPod.

4. Click on the name of the iPod in the Source list to select the iPod's music library, and drag songs from the iPod's song list to the playlist.

5. Click on the new playlist's name in the Source list, and drag songs to rearrange the list.

The order of songs in the playlist is based on the order in which you dragged them to the list. You rearrange the list by dragging songs within the playlist. To drag a song up the list and scroll at the same time, drag it over the up-arrow in the first column (the song number); to drag it down the list and scroll, drag it to the bottom of the list. You can drag a group of songs at once by selecting them (using click and Shift-click or Command-click).

 TIP

You can copy songs directly to your iPod by copying them into iPod playlists. Click the iTunes music library (the top name in the Source list) rather than the iPod music library (the iPod name) so that you can drag songs directly from the iTunes Library to an iPod playlist.

With the iPod Library open in iTunes, you can edit song information just like you do in the iTunes Library by scrolling down the song list and selecting songs.

You can edit the Song Name, Artist, Album, Genre, and My Ratings fields right in the song list. To edit song information, select the text and type over it. It may be easier, however, to edit this information by choosing File>Get Info and typing the text into the Song Information window.

To change a group of songs at once (for example, to change the artist name so that the last name appears first, as in "Garcia, Jerry"), follow these steps:

1. Select a group of songs. To select a range of songs, click on the first song, and then hold down the Shift key while clicking on the last song. You can add to a selection by holding down the Command key when clicking another song.

2. Choose File>Get Info, or press Command-I. The Get Info command displays a warning message when you have selected multiple songs: "Are you sure you want to edit information for multiple items?" Be careful with this editing procedure. If, for example, you change the song name, the entire selection will then have that song name. I recommend leaving the warning option "Do not ask me again" unchecked so that the warning appears whenever you try this.

3. Click Yes to edit information for multiple items. The Multiple Song Information window appears.

4. Edit the text fields for the multiple songs.

When you edit a field, a check mark appears automatically in the box next to the field. This is because iTunes assumes you want that field to be changed throughout the song selection. The check mark indicates that the field will be changed when you click OK. Before doing that, first make sure no other box is checked except the Artist field. Then click OK to make the change.

While the track information grabbed from the Internet is usually enough, it is by no means complete, nor does it match your personal taste with its choices for genre. Some facts, such as composer credits, may not be included in the information grabbed from the Internet. However, composer information is important for iPod users, because the iPod lets you scroll music by composer as well as by artist, album, and song. If you have the time and inclination to add composer credits, it is worth your while because you can then search, sort, and create playlists based on this information.

Editing in MusicMatch Jukebox

In MusicMatch Jukebox, you can add playlists directly to the iPod and rearrange songs within them. The iPod's playlists appear directly under the iPod's name on the left side of the PortablesPlus window. The contents of the iPod (or the contents of the selected playlist in the iPod) appear in the right side of the window.

To add a new playlist directly on the iPod:

1. Connect your iPod to your PC, and wait for it to be recognized by MusicMatch Jukebox. Your iPod should appear in the PortablesPlus window under the Attached Portable Devices folder. If the window is not yet open, choose File>Send to Portable Device.

2. Select the iPod so that its contents appear in the right side of the window.

3. Click the Add (+) button at the bottom-right side of the window to add a new playlist to the iPod, and give the new playlist a name.

4. Drag a selection of songs from the iPod song list to the playlist window.

5. Click the Save button, and give the playlist a name.

6. Drag the playlist's name from below the MusicMatch Jukebox Playlists folder in the right side of the PortablesPlus window to the iPod's name so that a + symbol appears, allowing you to copy the playlist to the iPod.

The order of songs in the playlist is based on the order in which you dragged them to the list. You can reorder the list by dragging songs within the playlist. To reorder the songs in a playlist on the iPod:

1. Select the iPod's playlist so that its contents appear in the right side of the window.

2. Right-click (use the alternate mouse button) to show the pop-up menu, and choose Reorder Playlist, as shown in Figure 3.46.

3. Drag the songs into the order you want for the playlist, as shown in Figure 3.47.

Backing Up and Sharing Your Music Library

Copyright law, and common sense, prohibits you from copying a commercial CD and selling the copy to someone else. You also can't sell the individual songs of a commercial CD. However, you *are* allowed to make copies of music for your personal use, including copies for your iPod and for backup purposes.

Some music that you can use with your iPod is protected. The Apple Music Store uses technology that protects the rights of artists, while also giving consumers some leeway in how they can use the music. You can copy the music files freely, so file backup is easy and straightforward on either a PC or a Mac.

FIGURE 3.46   *Selecting a playlist on the iPod using MusicMatch Jukebox, and choosing Reorder Playlist.*

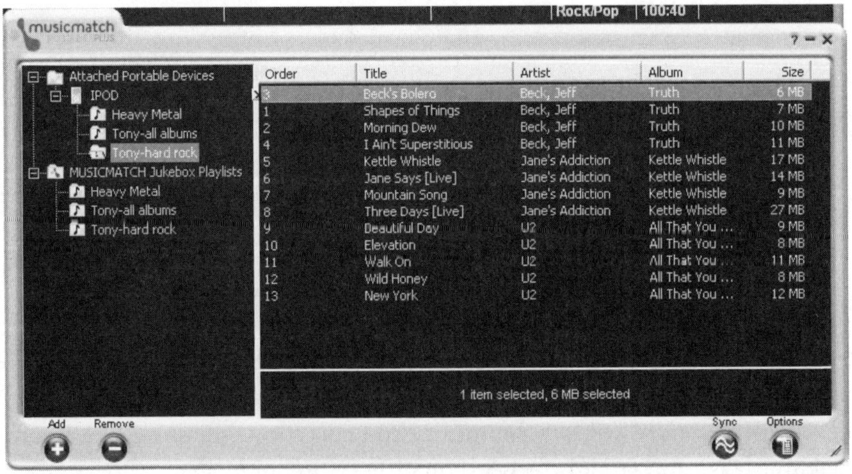

FIGURE 3.47   *Reordering the songs in a playlist on the iPod using MusicMatch Jukebox.*

On a Mac, you can also share the music with other Macs to a limited extent. You can play a song on up to three Macs, which you can "authorize" and "de-authorize" as you wish, so you can continue to upgrade your computers and protect your music investment. You can even share a music library over a home network of Macs, such as Apple's wireless AirPort network, so that everyone on the network can play the music.

Whether or not you are used to managing files on your hard disk, you may want to know where these songs are stored, so that you can copy music to other computers and make a backup of the entire library. You may also want to move the library to another computer.

Music files created by either iTunes or MusicMatch Jukebox can be copied freely from one hard drive to another and from one computer to another, and even from one type of computer to another type of computer. Music files in the MP3 and WAV formats can be used on both Macs and PCs as well as Linux machines.

iTunes Library Backup and Sharing

iTunes manages its library by copying music files to a central location. While you can link to music files located anywhere on your hard disk, you would want to consolidate your music library anyway, by copying music files to one folder, so that you can easily back up or copy everything to another computer. By consolidating your library first, you make sure that your backup is complete.

Normally iTunes imports all music to your iTunes Music folder, located inside your iTunes folder. The path to this folder is typically *your home folder*/Music/iTunes/ iTunes Music. iTunes makes a copy of any songs you drag to the iTunes window and stores the copy in the iTunes Music folder as well.

You could also have music in your library that is not actually in your library at all— it could be "streamed" to your computer over the Internet, or it might be part of a shared library or playlist on a network.

You can find out the location of any song by selecting the song and choosing File>Get Info, then clicking the Summary tab to see the Summary pane. If the "Kind" section of the Summary pane says "remote," then the song is not on your hard disk. You can also see the location of the music file at the very bottom of the Summary pane in the "Where" section. If you have songs in different locations— on different hard disks connected to the same Mac, or shared over a network—you can have iTunes consolidate your music library by copying everything into the iTunes Music Library folder.

To consolidate your music library, copying any remote songs to your hard disk, choose Advanced>Consolidate Library. The original songs remain where they are, but copies are made in your music folder.

To copy your music library to another disk, locate the iTunes folder using the Finder. It is usually located within the Music folder in your home folder (*your home folder/ Music/iTunes*). Drag this entire folder to another hard disk or backup device, and you're all set.

If you subscribe to Apple's .Mac service, you can use its hassle-free Backup software. With Backup, which comes with a .Mac membership, you can quickly and easily store important files on your iDisk. Backup allows you to save the latest versions of your files regularly and automatically, so you'll never have to worry about losing songs or any other important documents. When you use Backup, select the iTunes folder, which is usually within the Music folder in your home folder. You can perform the backup operation immediately or schedule automatic backups to occur at some other time.

To copy your entire music library to another Mac (for example, from an "old" one to a "new" one), follow these steps:

1. If there is a music library with music in the "new" Mac, move the music folders inside the iTunes Music folder to another folder, or copy them to another disk and delete them. If the music library is empty, you can skip this step and delete it or replace it during the next step.

2. Copy the iTunes Music folder from the "old" Mac to the iTunes folder of the "new" Mac. This folder is inside the iTunes folder of the "old" Mac, and should be copied to the same folder of the "new" Mac. You can replace the old one if it is empty. This folder contains all the music files.

3. Choose File>Export Library to export the file "Library.xml" from the iTunes folder of the "old" Mac, and copy "Library.xml" to the "new" Mac, using any folder other than the iTunes folder. When you export your entire library, iTunes creates an XML file called "Library.xml" that contains all the playlist information and links to music files.

4. Start iTunes on the "new" Mac. Choose File>Import, and import the "Library.xml" file.

You can copy songs freely from your iTunes Music folder to other folders, other disks, and other computers. The files are organized in folders by artist name, and by album, within the iTunes Music folder, so it is easy to copy an entire album or every song by a specific artist. You can find out the location of any song by selecting the song and choosing File>Get Info, then clicking the Summary tab to see the Summary pane.

TIP

The song information that accompanies each song can't be copied in this fashion. But you can export a playlist of the songs by creating the playlist, selecting the playlist, and choosing File>Export Song List, picking XML from the Format pop-up menu. When you export a playlist you get a list of songs in the XML (Extensible Markup Language) format with the song information. You can then import the playlist into another computer by choosing File>Import and selecting the XML file.

If you use your Mac on a wireless or wired network, you can share the music in your library with up to five other computers in the same network. With one Mac designated as the "library Mac", the other Macs on the network can find and play music in the shared library.

When you use a computer on the network to play a song on the library Mac, the song is *streamed* from the library Mac to your computer over the network—it is not copied to your music library. From your computer, you can't burn onto CD, or copy to an iPod, songs that are shared on the library Mac. You can, of course, do those things on the library Mac.

You can share radio links, MP3, AIFF, and WAV files, and even AAC files and music purchased from the Apple Music Store, but not Audible spoken word files or QuickTime sound files. If you have a large network (such as an office network), check to make sure the computers share the same subnet. The computers need to be within the same subnet to share music.

To share your music library, turning your Mac into the "library" Mac, follow these steps:

1. Choose iTunes>Preferences and click the Sharing button.
2. Click the option to "Share my music."
3. Click to "Share entire library" or "Share selected playlists" and select the playlists to share.
4. Type a name for the shared library, and add a password if you want. The name will appear in the Source list for other computers that share it. The password restricts access to those who know it.

On the other computers on the network, you can share the music by following these steps:

1. Choose iTunes>Preferences and click the Sharing button (requires Mac OS X 10.2.4 or newer).

2. Click the option to "Look for shared music." The shared libraries or playlists appear in your iTunes Source list under the name used for sharing it.

3. Click on the shared library or playlist to play it.

Up to five other Macs on the network can enjoy the music in your library. This can be incredibly useful for playing music on laptops like PowerBooks that support the wireless AirPort network. You could put all your music on one computer and use it throughout the network.

MusicMatch Jukebox Music Libraries

MusicMatch Jukebox stores music files created from recording CDs in folders inside the My Music folder in your Documents folder, unless you specify otherwise. The path to this folder is typically *your home folder*/My Documents/My Music, and inside this folder are folders organized by artist name.

MusicMatch Jukebox libraries are actually collections of links to music files. Those files can be anywhere on your hard disk, not just in your music folder inside your documents folder. You can maintain multiple libraries as well, without using much disk space, because each library is essentially a playlist. You could also have music in your library that is not actually on your hard disk at all—it could be "streamed" to your computer over the Internet and never actually stored in a music file on your disk.

It is therefore time-consuming to consolidate all these files in one place for easy backup. The best way is to use disk backup software that copies all your files, or to selectively copy the music files as you see fit. You can find out the location of any song's music file by selecting the song and right-clicking (using the alternate mouse button) to show the pop-up menu, and choosing Open File Location.

Music libraries are essentially links to music files organized with playlist information and other text (mostly song information), and can be saved as separate library files as well as exported in a text database format. To save a music library, choose Options>Music Library>Save Music Library As. MusicMatch Jukebox saves the file with the filename extension ".ddf", as in "yourlibrary.ddf", which is the MusicMatch Jukebox-specific format for music library files. You can save as many different music libraries as you want, such as libraries dedicated to specific types of music or libraries associated with different people.

To load a saved music library, choose Options>Music Library>Open Music Library, and browse for the saved music library, which should have the ".ddf" extension. You can also import an entire music library into another music library, combining the two libraries, by choosing Options>Music Library>Import Music Library.

If you have moved your music files or renamed any folders in the path to your music files, and MusicMatch Jukebox can't find the music file associated with a song, choose Options>Music Library>Repair Broken Links, and browse to the folder where the music file now resides.

You now know all you need to know about organizing and managing music libraries for use with your iPod. The next chapter provides more in-depth information about music file encoding and compression options, and equalizer usage, in order to get higher quality sound for your music while also saving disk space.

Chapter 4

Tweaking
the Sound

Here's what you'll explore in this chapter:

- ◆ Getting the best sound quality *and* the most efficient use of disk space when ripping CDs.
- ◆ Using the advanced options for encoding formats in iTunes and MusicMatch Jukebox.
- ◆ Converting songs from one encoding format to another.
- ◆ Recording audio from analog sources such as phonograph turntables and tape decks.
- ◆ Assigning equalizer presets to songs for use when playing back on the iPod.

The iPod faithfully reproduces whatever you put into it. The music you play on the iPod is exactly the same as the music in your computer's library, which in turn is only as good as the source recording and the importing settings you used.

This chapter provides more information about the audio compression settings used to rip CDs and import music. You may be quite happy with the results using the default settings. But listening pleasure depends entirely on the listener, and some people can hear qualitative differences that others don't hear or don't care about.

You can specify the audio compression settings to your liking. You may want to import music at average-quality settings that allow you to put more songs on your hard disk and iPod than if you chose higher-quality settings. Or you may be picky about the sound quality and, with an ear that anticipates future generations of iPods and cheap hard disks, decide to trade space for quality. You might therefore import music at the highest possible quality and then convert the songs to lower-quality, space-saving copies for the iPod.

This chapter also provides suggested settings for importing sounds other than music, tips on converting songs from one format to another, and methods of enhancing music with the built-in equalizer, as well as saving equalizer settings with songs.

Compression and Encoding Formats

Ripping music from a CD is a process of compressing the song's digital information and encoding it in a particular sound file format. Ripping is a straightforward process, but the settings you choose for importing affect sound quality, disk space (and iPod space), and compatibility with other types of players and computers.

Compression reduces the sound quality because it throws away information to make the file smaller. The amount the file is reduced depends on the bit rate you choose, as well as the encoding format and other options. More compression means more space is available in your iPod for more music files, but the music quality is poorer. Less compression means better quality and larger music files that take up more space in your iPod.

Power is also an issue. In iPods, playing larger files takes up more power because the hard disk inside the iPod has to refresh its memory buffers more quickly to process more information as the song plays. You can therefore trade quality for space to have more music and play your iPod longer with its battery. Or you can trade space for quality, and have higher-quality music with less space, and less time with your iPod battery.

Everyone hears the effects of compression differently. For some, music that is overly compressed may sound tinny, lacking in depth, and even distorted in places where the sound is loud. For others, compression offers the capability of adding many more albums to an iPod, and they can't hear the difference.

But too much compression can be a bad thing. Further compressing an already-compressed music file—by converting a song, as described later in this chapter—reduces the quality significantly, which is why you should convert only uncompressed songs. And once your song is compressed, it can never be uncompressed back to its original quality. Your song is essentially locked into that encoding format.

How Compression Works

Audio compression methods throw away digital information using what are known as *lossy* (as opposed to loss-less) compression algorithms. Lossy compression loses information each time you use it, which means that if you compress something that was already compressed, you lose more information than before.

Encoding formats such as MP3 and AAC use two basic methods to compress audio: removing non-audible frequencies and removing the less important signals.

For non-audible frequencies, the compression removes what you supposedly can't hear. For example, if a background singer is drowned out by a rhythm guitar, and it is nearly impossible to hear the singer because of the intensity of the guitar's sound, the compression algorithm removes the singer's sound while maintaining the guitar's sound, reducing the amount of information needed to reproduce the sound you *can* hear.

Within the sound spectrum of frequencies that can be heard by humans, some frequencies are considered less important in terms of rendering fidelity, and some that most people can't hear at all. Removing specific frequencies is likely to be less damaging to your music than other types of compression, depending on how you hear things.

Overview of Encoding Formats

If convenience is the issue, and you want to put as many albums onto your hard disk and iPod as you can, you can trade just a little bit of quality for a lot of space using encoded formats that offer compression, such as MP3 and AAC. As an iPod user, you gain an additional benefit: smaller music files use less battery power.

For Mac users, I recommend AAC, which is supported by iTunes. For PC users who don't have AAC, I recommend the standard MP3 encoder, or if you want even smaller files, the special mp3PRO encoder, both provided with MusicMatch Jukebox.

If you intend your computer music library to have the best possible quality, you might consider not using compression at all, and not compromising on quality. You could import music at the highest possible quality—uncompressed AIFF or WAV—and then convert the music files to a lesser-quality format for use in the iPod. For example, on a Mac I use AIFF exclusively for music I intend to burn onto a CD, then either re-import or convert the music to AAC for use in my iPod. On a PC I use WAV for music I intend to burn onto a CD, then either re-record or convert the music to MP3 for my iPod.

The following are descriptions of all the audio encoding formats supported by the iPod, and by iTunes and MusicMatch Jukebox:

◆ **AAC:** Apple's new music file format, known as MPEG-4 Advanced Audio Coding, is a higher quality format than MP3, comparable to CD quality.

(MPEG stands for Moving Pictures Experts Group, a body that recognizes compression standards for video and audio.) AAC offers the best tradeoff of space and quality. All your purchased music from the Apple Music Store comes in this format. It is also suitable (though not as good as AIFF) for burning to an audio CD, and excellent for playing in an iPod or from hard disk. However, as of this writing it is supported only by iTunes.

◆ **AIFF:** The Audio Interchange File Format is the standard digital format for uncompressed sound on a Mac, and it provides the highest quality representation of the sound. Use AIFF if you plan on burning the song to an audio CD. Mac-based digital sound editing programs import and export AIFF files, and you can edit and save in AIFF with absolutely no loss in quality. AIFF files take up large amounts of disk and iPod space because they're uncompressed.

◆ **MP3:** The MPEG-1, Layer 3 format, also known as MP3, is supported everywhere. (MPEG stands for Moving Pictures Experts Group, a body that recognizes compression standards for video and audio.) Use the MP3 format for songs you intend to send to others or use with MP3 players. The MP3 format offers quite a lot of different compression and quality settings, so you can fine-tune the format to get better quality, sacrificing disk (and iPod) space as you dial up the quality. Use the MP3 format for a song you intend to burn on an MP3 CD. (AIFF or WAV are better for regular audio CDs.)

◆ **mp3PRO:** This special encoder provided with MusicMatch Jukebox creates an MP3 file as described above, only smaller. Use the mp3PRO encoder for even greater file compression than with the standard MP3 encoder. The mp3PRO encoder is typically used for songs that don't require extreme high-fidelity playback, as it compresses files even further and allows more songs to fit in your iPod.

◆ **WAV:** Waveform Audio File Format is a digital audio standard that Windows-based PCs can understand and manipulate. Like AIFF, WAV is uncompressed and provides the highest quality representation of the sound. Use WAV if you plan on burning the song to an audio CD or using it with PC-based digital sound editing programs, which import and export WAV files. WAV files take up large amounts of disk and iPod space because they're uncompressed.

NOTE

Other digital formats for sound include DVD-Audio (DVD-A) and Super Audio CD (SACD). DVD-Audio is a relatively new format developed from DVD video and based on PCM (pulse code modulation) recording technology, but it offers improved sound quality over PCM by using a higher sampling frequency and longer word lengths. iTunes and MusicMatch Jukebox do not yet support the DVD-Audio format, but you can import a digital video file containing DVD-Audio sound into iMovie or another digital video editing program, extract the sound, and export the sound in AIFF or WAV format, which can be used with iTunes or MusicMatch Jukebox.

The Super Audio CD is a new format developed from the past audio format for CDs. The SACD format is based on Direct Stream Digital (DSD) recording technology that closely reproduces the shape of the original analog waveforms to produce a more natural, higher quality sound. Originally developed for the digital archiving of priceless analogue masters tapes, DSD is based on 1-bit sigma-delta modulation, and operates with a sampling frequency of 2.8224 MHz (i.e., 64 times the 44.1 kHz used in audio CDs). Philips and Sony have adopted DSD as the basis for SACD, and the format is growing in popularity among audiophiles. However, iTunes and MusicMatch Jukebox do not support SACD. If you buy music product in the SACD format, choose the "hybrid" format that offers a conventional CD layer and a high-density SACD layer. You can then import the music from the conventional CD layer.

iTunes Importing and Converting Options

Before you rip an audio CD or convert a sound file, you should first set the importing preferences in iTunes to the encoding format, bit rate, and quality settings you want.

Setting Importing Preferences

In iTunes, choose iTunes>Preferences, and then click the Importing button at the top of the window. The Encoder pop-up menu lets you choose an encoding format. The Setting pop-up menu offers different settings depending on your choice of encoder. As shown in Figure 4.1, the AAC Encoder offers only two choices: High Quality and Custom. To fine-tune the AAC Encoder settings, choose Custom.

Use the pop-up menus in the AAC Encoder preferences window, as shown in Figure 4.2, and then click OK to accept your changes. From that point on, until you change the settings again, iTunes remembers the settings you specified and uses them whenever it imports.

FIGURE 4.1 *Choosing the Custom setting for the AAC encoder in the iTunes Import preferences.*

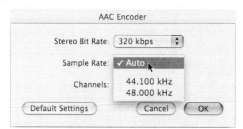

FIGURE 4.2 *Choosing the Auto setting for the sample rate in the AAC Encoder preferences in iTunes.*

Read the section below on the AAC Encoder Options for information about these settings.

Converting Songs to Other Formats

If you want to get the benefits of different formats, you can import a CD using one encoder, then import it again using a different encoder. However, it may be faster to import at the highest possible quality in uncompressed AIFF or WAV, and then convert the music files to a lesser-quality format for use in the iPod or other devices. You can do this because AIFF and WAV do not compress the music, so the conversion process compresses only once.

WARNING

Converting a song from a compressed format to another compressed format is possible, but you may not like the results. When you convert a compressed file (such as those encoded as ACC or MP3) to another compressed format, the music is compressed twice, reducing the quality of the sound. It is better to start with an uncompressed song, imported using either the AIFF or WAV format, and convert that to the compressed AAC or MP3 format.

When you convert a song, iTunes creates a copy and converts the copy to the new format, so that the original remains intact in its original format. Both versions appear in your music library. You can tell which one's which by selecting one of them and choosing File>Get Info. The Summary button displays the "Kind" of music file and the "Format."

WARNING

You can't convert songs purchased from the Apple Music Store, because they are encoded as protected AAC files.

To convert a song to another format using iTunes, follow these steps:

1. Choose iTunes>Preferences, and then click the Importing button. The Importing button displays the Importing preferences, where you can make changes to the encoding format and its settings.

2. Choose the encoding format you want to convert the song into, and the settings for that format. For example, you may be converting songs in the AIFF format to the MP3 format. You would choose the MP3 format and its settings.

3. Select one or more songs, and choose Advanced>Convert Selection.

In iTunes, the encoding format you chose in Step 2 appears in the menu: Convert Selection to MP3, Convert Selection to AAC, Convert Selection to AIFF, or Convert Selection to WAV.

This automatic copy-and-convert operation can be useful for converting an entire music library to another format. In iTunes, hold down the Option key and choose Advanced>Convert Selection, and all the songs are copied and converted automatically. If you have a library of AIFF tunes, you can quickly copy and convert them to AAC or MP3 in one step, and then assign the AIFF songs to the AIFF-associated playlists for burning CDs, and MP3 or AAC songs to MP3 or AAC playlists that you intend to copy to your iPod.

AAC Encoder Options

When you choose the AAC Encoder, the Setting pop-up menu offers only two choices: High Quality and Custom. To fine-tune the AAC Encoder settings, choose Custom. The custom settings for AAC let you change the stereo bit rate, the sample rate, and the number of channels.

Stereo bit rate: The stereo bit rate is measured in kilobits per second (kbps). Use a higher bit rate for higher quality, which has the side effect of increasing the file size. The most common bit rate for AAC files is 128 kbps. Lower bit rates are more appropriate for voice recordings or sound effects. I recommend at least 192 kbps for most music, and I use 320 kbps, the maximum setting, for songs I play on my iPod.

Sample rate: The sample rate is the number of times per second the sound waveform is captured digitally ("sampled"). Higher sample rates yield higher quality sound and large file sizes. However, you should never use a higher sample rate than the rate used for the source—CDs use a 44.1 kHz rate, so choosing a higher rate is unnecessary, unless you are converting a song that was recorded from DAT (at 48 kHz) or directly into the Mac at a high sample rate, and you want to keep that sample rate.

Channels: Stereo, which offers two channels of music for left and right speakers, is the norm for music. Mono, a.k.a. monaural or single-channel, was the norm for pop records before the mid-1960s. Monaural recordings take up half the space of stereo recordings when digitized. Choose Auto to use the appropriate setting that matches the source.

MP3 Encoder Options

The MP3 Encoder in iTunes offers four choices for Setting:

Good Quality (128 kbps): This setting is fine for audio books, comedy records, other voice recordings, and old scratchy records. You may even want to go lower in bit rate (kbps stands for kilobits per second).

High Quality (160 kbps): Most people consider this high enough for most popular music.

Higher Quality (192 kbps): High enough for just about all types of music.

Custom: To fine-tune the MP3 Encoder settings, choose Custom to make changes to the MP3 Encoder preferences, as shown in Figure 4.3.

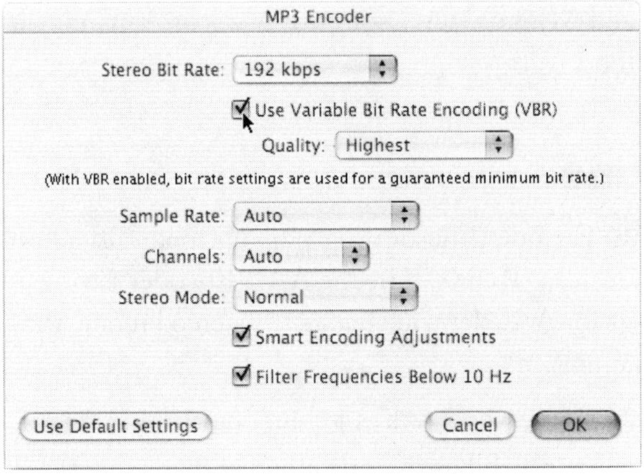

FIGURE 4.3 *Choosing settings for the MP3 Encoder preferences in iTunes.*

The MP3 Encoder offers a raft of settings in its custom settings window. Customizing your MP3 settings may increase the sound quality while also keeping file size low.

Stereo bit rate: Measured in kilobits per second (kbps), use a higher bit rate for higher quality, which of course increases the file size. The most common bit rate for MP3 files you find on the Web is 128 kbps. Lower bit rates are more appropriate for voice recordings or sound effects. I recommend at least 192 kbps for most music, and I use 320 kbps, the maximum setting, for songs I play on my iPod.

Variable Bit Rate Encoding (VBR): This option varies the number of bits used to store the music depending on the complexity of the sound. If you use the Highest setting for VBR, iTunes encodes at up to the maximum bit rate of 320 kbps in sections of songs where the sound is complex enough to require a high bit rate, while keeping the rest of the song at a lower bit rate to save file space. The lower limit is set by the rate you chose in the Stereo Bit Rate pop-up menu, as shown in Figure 4.4

Sample rate: The sample rate is the number of times per second the sound waveform is captured digitally ("sampled"). Higher sample rates yield higher quality sound and large file sizes. However, you should never use a higher sample rate than the rate used for the source—CDs use a 44.1 kHz rate, so choosing a higher rate is unnecessary, unless you are converting a song that was recorded from DAT (48 kHz) or directly into the Mac at a high sample rate, and you want to keep that sample rate.

Channels: Stereo, which offers two channels of music for left and right speakers, is the norm for music. Mono, a.k.a. monaural or single-channel, was the norm for

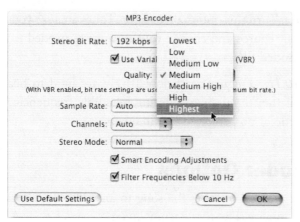

FIGURE 4.4 *Setting Variable Bit Rate Encoding for the MP3 Encoder preferences in iTunes.*

pop records before the mid-1960s. Monaural recordings take up half the space of stereo recordings when digitized. Choose Auto to use the appropriate setting that matches the source.

Stereo mode: Normal mode is normal stereo. Choose Joint Stereo, as shown in Figure 4.5, to make the file smaller by removing information that is identical in both channels of a stereo recording, using only one channel for that information, while the other channel carries unique information. At bit rates of 128 kbps and below, this mode can actually improve the sound quality.

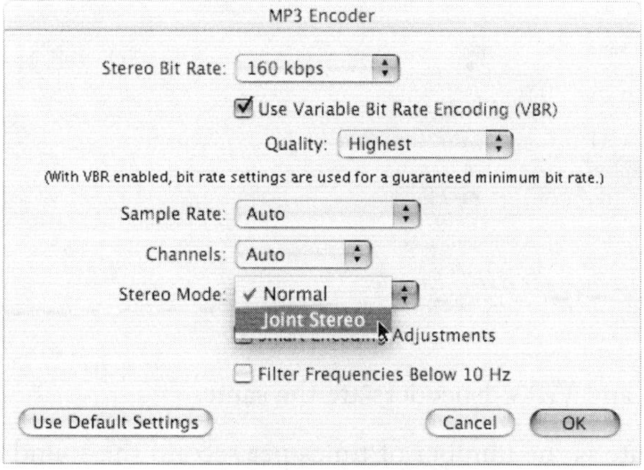

FIGURE 4.5 *Choosing Joint Stereo for the MP3 Encoder preferences in iTunes to reduce file size without affecting quality.*

Smart Encoding Adjustments: Turn this option on to have iTunes analyze your MP3 encoding settings and music source and change your settings as needed to maximize the quality of the encoded files.

Filter Frequencies Below 10 Hz: Frequencies below 10 Hz are hard to hear, and most people don't notice if they're missing. Filtering inaudible frequencies helps reduce the file size with little or no perceived loss in quality.

AIFF and WAV Encoder Options

Use AIFF or WAV if you plan on burning the song to an audio CD, because it offers the highest possible quality. The files occupy lots more space than AAC or MP3 files because they are not compressed.

The AIFF and WAV Encoders offer basically the same settings, including an Automatic setting that automatically sets the sample rate, sample size, and channels according to the source. You can choose Custom to change these settings, as shown in Figure 4.6.

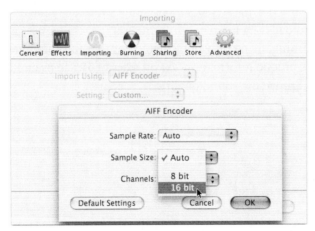

FIGURE 4.6   *Customizing the settings for AIFF Encoder preferences in iTunes.*

The options for the AIFF and WAV Encoders are the same:

Sample rate: The sample rate is the number of times per second the sound waveform is captured digitally ("sampled"). Higher sample rates yield higher quality sound and large file sizes. However, you should never use a higher sample rate than the rate used for the source—CDs use a 44.1 kHz rate, so choosing a higher rate is unnecessary, unless you are converting a song that was recorded from DAT (48 kHz) or directly into the Mac at a high sample rate, and you want to keep that sample rate. AIFF and WAV offer more choices in sample rates, down to a very low sample rate of 8 kHz suitable only for voice.

Sample size: The size of the "word" used to store each sample (captured waveform), which determines the overall sound quality of the sample. Audio CDs use a 16-bit sample size, and some voice recordings use only 8-bit. You should use 16-bit for music, or choose Auto to match the sample size of the source.

Channels: Stereo, which offers two channels of music for left and right speakers, is the norm for music. Mono, a.k.a. monaural or single-channel, was the norm for pop records before the mid-1960s. Monaural recordings take up half the space of stereo recordings when digitized. Choose Auto to use the appropriate setting that matches the source.

AIFF and WAV files are not compressed, so there is no loss in quality from the original source. However, the files are huge. The MP3 or AAC version of an AIFF or WAV song would be one-tenth the size on your hard disk and in your iPod.

MusicMatch JukeBox Recording and Converting Options

Before you rip an audio CD, you should first set the recording options in MusicMatch Jukebox to the encoding format and settings you want.

Setting Recording Options

MusicMatch Jukebox offers numerous recording options for fine-tuning the CD ripping process. To change your recording options, choose Options>Settings>Recorder, which displays the Recorder Settings window as shown in Figure 4.7. When you first use the program, the MP3 recording format is chosen by default, offering various quality options. You can change the recording format to mp3PRO, WAV, Windows Media, and other formats associated with third-party plug-in software for MusicMatch Jukebox.

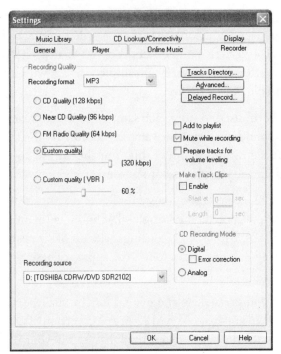

FIGURE 4.7   *Customizing the MP3-format recording settings for ripping CDs in MusicMatch Jukebox.*

MP3 Settings

You can choose the following preset quality settings for MP3 recording in MusicMatch Jukebox:

CD Quality (128 kbps): Measured in kilobits per second (kbps), this setting offers 128 kbps, the most common bit rate for MP3 files you find on the Web. The notion that this is "CD quality" is subjective, and I recommend at least 192 kbps for most music by choosing the Custom quality setting—I use 320 kbps, the maximum setting, for songs I play on my iPod. With this setting, one minute of music takes up about one megabyte of space.

Near CD Quality (96 kbps): This setting offers 96 kbps, and one minute of music takes up about 700 kilobytes. However, I find the quality to be poor. You may not hear the difference, and you can certainly cram more music on your iPod with this setting.

FM Radio Quality (64 kbps): Bit rates lower than 96 kbps are more appropriate for voice recordings or sound effects, not music. One minute takes up about 400 kilobytes.

Custom quality: This setting lets you set the stereo bit rate, measured in kilobits per second (kbps). A higher bit rate offers higher quality sound and increases the file size. The most common bit rate for MP3 files you find on the Web is 128 kbps. Lower bit rates are more appropriate for voice recordings or sound effects. I recommend at least 192 kbps for most music, and I use 320 kbps, the maximum setting, for songs I play on my iPod.

Custom quality (VBR): This setting uses Variable Bit Rate (VBR) encoding to vary the number of bits used to store the music depending on the complexity of the sound. MusicMatch Jukebox offers a range from 1 (lowest quality with highest compression) to 100 (highest quality with least compression). At its highest setting, VBR might use the highest bit rate of 320 kbps in sections of songs where the sound is complex enough to require a high bit rate, while keeping the rest of the song at a lower bit rate to save file space. I recommend using only the highest setting if you use VBR at all.

CD Recording Mode: MusicMatch Jukebox can record from a digital or analog source. When ripping CDs, use the *Digital* setting. You can also use the *Error correction* option to filter out noise and produce better results with CDs that have minor scratches. If you hear clicks and pops in the recorded digital music, or a jittery sound, try using this option, which minimizes the audio artifacts that occur from drive-seeking errors. Recording time takes longer but the recording quality may be better with some CD-ROM drives. The *Analog* setting, which records in real time, is by far the slowest method and is provided for recording from slow CD-ROM drives to get higher-quality results.

mp3PRO Settings

MusicMatch Jukebox also offers the mp3PRO encoder for creating smaller MP3 files that match in quality the larger files created by the default MP3 encoder. The mp3PRO encoder can create files that are nearly 50% smaller, but offers low bit rate settings up to only 96 kbps—use the MP3 encoder for higher bit rate settings.

CD Transparency (96 kbps): Measured in kilobits per second (kbps), this setting offers 96 kbps, which is lower than MP3 files you find on the Web, but many can't tell the difference. With this setting, one minute of music takes up about 600 kilobytes of space.

CD Quality (64 kbps): This setting offers 64 kbps, and one minute of music takes up about 300 kilobytes. However, I find the quality to be poor. You may not hear the difference, and you can certainly cram more music on your iPod with this set-ting. (The notion that this is "CD quality" is subjective. While many can't hear the difference, I would not refer to this bit rate setting as "CD quality.")

Superior FM Radio Quality (40 kbps): Bit rates lower than 96 kbps are more appro-priate for voice recordings or sound effects, not music. One minute takes up less than 300 kilobytes.

Custom quality: This setting lets you set the stereo bit rate, measured in kilobits per second (kbps). A higher bit rate offers higher quality sound and increases the file size. While most common bit rate for MP3 files you find on the Web is 128 kbps, the mp3PRO encoder offers 96 kbps as the highest rate—use the MP3 encoder for higher bit rates.

Custom quality (VBR): This setting uses Variable Bit Rate (VBR) encoding to vary the number of bits used to store the music depending on the complexity of the sound. MusicMatch Jukebox offers a range from 1 (lowest quality with highest compression) to 100 (highest quality with least compression). At its highest set-ting, VBR might use the highest bit rate in sections of songs where the sound is complex enough to require a high bit rate, while keeping the rest of the song at a lower bit rate to save file space. I recommend using only the highest setting if you use VBR at all.

CD Recording Mode: MusicMatch Jukebox can record from a digital or analog source. When ripping CDs, use the *Digital* setting. You can also use the *Error correction* option to filter out noise and produce better results with CDs that have minor scratches. If you hear clicks and pops in the recorded digital music, or a jittery sound, try using this option, which minimizes the audio artifacts that occur from drive-seeking errors. Recording time takes longer but the recording quality may be better with some CD-ROM drives. The *Analog* setting, which records in real time, is by far the slowest method and is provided for recording from slow CD-ROM drives to get higher-quality results.

WAV Settings

Use WAV if you plan on burning the song to an audio CD, because it offers the highest possible quality. The files occupy lots more space than MP3 files because they are not compressed. One minute of music in the WAV format occupies about 10 megabytes of disk/iPod space. CD Quality is the only option for WAV.

Advanced MP3 Settings

MusicMatch Jukebox offers advanced settings, available by clicking the Advanced button in the Settings window (shown in Figure 4.7). The Advanced Recording Options window appears, as shown in Figure 4.8.

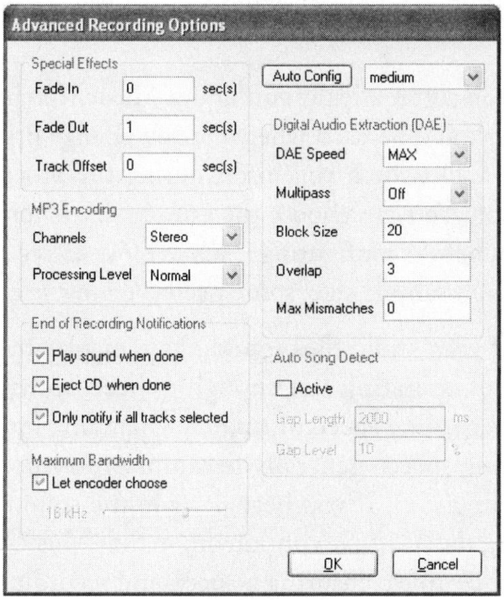

FIGURE 4.8   *Setting advanced recording options for ripping CDs in MusicMatch Jukebox.*

Use the Advanced Recording Options window to set a variety of recording options and special effects. The following options improve the recording quality while ripping songs from CDs:

MP3 Encoding: You can force recording into *Stereo* or *Mono* formats with this option. Stereo, which offers two channels of music for left and right speakers, is the norm for music. Mono, a.k.a. monaural or single-channel, was the norm for pop records before the mid-1960s. Monaural recordings take up half the space of stereo recordings when digitized. By default, MusicMatch Jukebox is set to use the appropriate setting that matches the source—*Stereo* for stereo sources, and *Mono* for mono sources.

Maximum Bandwidth: This option sets the range of frequencies allowed in the MP3 file. Within the sound spectrum of frequencies that can be heard by humans, some frequencies are considered less important in terms of rendering fidelity, and some that most people can't hear at all. The human ear can theoretically hear frequencies up to 22 kHz, but many humans can't really hear anything above 16 kHz. If you want frequencies higher than 16 kHz (often found in classical music), you can adjust this slider up. Note that this setting might raise the level of audio artifacts, such as scratches or surface imperfections in vinyl LPs, as well as slightly increase the file size.

Auto Config: The Auto Config button automatically configures MusicMatch Jukebox for your CD-ROM drive and should be used whenever you change drives. It samples data from a typical audio CD (which you insert during the process) in order to determine the configuration. You can choose the sample size (short, medium, or long) in the pop-up menu before configuring—while most drives can be configured using the short or medium sample size, some need the long size.

Digital Audio Extraction (DAE): If your audio files sound like they play too fast, it may be due to your CD drive not operating fast enough to keep up with the recording process—a drive speed/recording speed mismatch. Changing the *DAE Speed* setting to 4 (for a 4x recording speed) generally fixes this problem; if not, you can try 2x or real-time recording (1x). If you hear jitter in the sound, even with error correction on, try turning the *Multipass* option on, so that MusicMatch Jukebox reads the CD track multiple times, ensuring a successful recording (but also increasing recording time). You can also increase *Block Size* up to 100 to see if that helps reduce jitter and speed problems. If you hear artifacts such as pops and clicks as well as jitter, you can increase *Overlap* up to 10. This improves the recording process by collecting additional frames of audio information before and after a specific block of information, to ensure that the specific block is accurate. The Max Mismatches, or maximum number of mismatched blocks, can be increased to 255 when a recording still has jitter, artifacts, or inconsistent speed, in order to enhance MusicMatch Jukebox's ability to stitch together bad blocks. Most of these options tend to slow down the recording process in order to improve the quality of the recording.

The following are special effects you may want to use while recording songs.

Fade In: You can record a song with a fade-in at the beginning, if you wish, with the number of seconds for the fade-in. The fade-in is recorded along with the audio, so it is permanently part of the music file. This option is useful if the song begins with the sound of an audience clapping, or some other noise heard before the music begins.

Fade Out: You can record a song with a fade-out at the end, if you wish, with the number of seconds for the fade-out. The fade-out is recorded along with the audio, so it is permanently part of the music file. This option is useful if the song ends with the sound of an audience clapping and you want to fade out the audience earlier than the track ends.

Track Offset: Use this option to start the recording process a number of seconds into the track, not at the very beginning. For example, if a CD track has no sound or an introduction that you want to skip, you can specify the number of seconds to skip (a.k.a. *offset*) before starting to record. By combining the Fade In, Fade Out, and Track Offset options, you could record only a portion of a long CD track and have the extracted portion fade in and out properly.

Converting Songs to Other Formats

If you want to get the benefits of different formats, you can import a CD using one encoder, such as WAV, then import it again using a different encoder, such as MP3. However, it may be faster to import at the highest possible quality in uncompressed WAV, and then convert the music files to a lesser-quality format for use in the iPod or other devices. You can do this because the WAV format, like Apple's AIFF format, does not compress the music, so the conversion process compresses only once.

WARNING

Converting a song from a compressed format to another compressed format is possible, but you may not like the results. When you convert a compressed file (such as those encoded as MP3) to another compressed format, the music is compressed twice, reducing the quality of the sound. It is better to start with an uncompressed song, imported using the WAV format, and convert that to the compressed MP3 format.

To convert one or more songs to another format in MusicMatch Jukebox, follow these steps:

1. Choose File>Convert to open the File Format Conversion window as shown in Figure 4.9.

2. Select the format of the source files using the Source Data Type pop-up menu. Typically you would convert WAV files, so the source format should be WAV.

3. In the Source Directory pane, in the top-left portion of the window, browse to the folder containing the source files.

4. Select the music files to convert in the Highlight Files to Convert pane, which lists all the music files in the folder you selected that match the format you selected (for example, all the WAV files). You can click on each filename, or use the Select All button to select all of them.

5. In the Destination Directory pane in the top-right portion of the window browse to the folder that should contain the newly converted songs. If you want to use a new folder for these songs, create the folder first using Windows Explorer.

6. Select the format of the destination files using the Destination Data Type pop-up menu. Typically you would convert from WAV to MP3, so the destination format should be MP3.

7. When converting songs to MP3, you can adjust the slider for the bit rate up to 320 kbps to adjust the quality of the MP3 song. Measured in kilobits per second (kbps), use a higher bit rate for higher quality, which of course

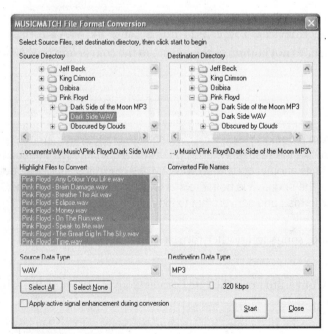

FIGURE 4.9 *Converting songs from the WAV format to the MP3 format in MusicMatch Jukebox.*

increases the file size. The most common bit rate for MP3 files on the Web is 128 kbps. Lower bit rates are more appropriate for voice recordings or sound effects. I recommend at least 192 kbps for most music, and I use 320 kbps, the maximum setting, for songs I play on my iPod.

8. Click the Start button to start the conversion process. A progress window shows you the progress of the operation.

While MusicMatch Jukebox lets you convert MP3 to WAV, or an MP3 at a lower bit rate to an MP3 with a higher bit rate, neither conversion improves song quality. You may have a reason for converting MP3 to WAV, but the song's quality remains exactly the same as the MP3 version while taking up lots more space as a WAV file. The same is true about converting MP3s from one-bit rate to a higher rate—the song remains at the same quality level but takes up more disk space. The most useful conversion is from WAV (the format used for burning CDs) to MP3 (the format used on the Web and iPod); this conversion reduces the quality of the song slightly, but shrinks the file size exponentially, so that more songs can fit on your iPod.

Line-In Recording

You may want to bring music into your computer directly from an analog source, such as a turntable for playing vinyl records, or stereo microphones for recording live directly into the computer.

To do this, you need a way to connect the analog source to your computer through a line-in connection—typically a stereo mini-jack on your sound card or computer, which accepts a standard stereo mini-plug cable. Your mini-plug cable may connect to the analog source device (such as an amplifier or mixer) using RCA-type left and right stereo plugs or a stereo mini-plug.

On a Mac, you can use the Mac's line-in or microphone-in connector and the Sound Studio program, found in the Applications folder in Mac OS X systems. (You can use it for about 2 weeks before paying for it.) On a PC, you can use the line-in or mic-in connector on your sound card, and the Record Line-In function in MusicMatch Jukebox.

When recording from a phonograph (turntable for vinyl records), the phonograph must either include an amplifier or be connected to an amplifier, in order to raise the signal to line levels and apply proper RIAA equalization curves.

Before recording directly into your computer, be sure you have enough disk space to record the audio in an uncompressed form. If you are recording an hour of music, you will need about 600 megabytes of disk space to record it. You can convert the sound file into a compressed format (such as MP3) using iTunes or MusicMatch Jukebox after recording.

Macintosh Line-In Recording

To record directly into your Mac from either a home stereo system or through a microphone (either the Mac's built-in microphone, an external microphone that connects to the Mac, or a USB microphone that connects through the Mac's USB port), you can use Sound Studio, which is available free for a two-week trial period. For newer Macs that no longer have the line-in connections, you can purchase a USB audio input device such as the Griffin iMic or the Roland UA-30.

First, set the volume for the recording. Open the Mac's Sound panel in System Preferences, and click the Input tab to see the sound input preferences, as shown in Figure 4.10. You can record using the Mac's internal microphone, or choose Line In.

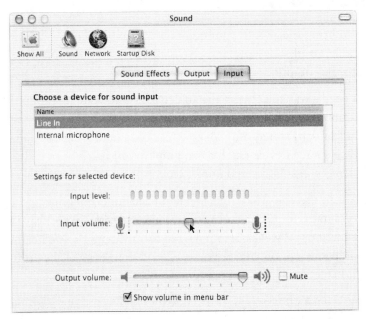

FIGURE 4.10 *Setting the sound input device (line in) and input volume for recording directly into a Macintosh.*

Next, open Sound Studio and choose Audio>Sound Input/Output Setup. The Sound Input/Output Setup window, shown in Figure 4.11, lets you choose the input device and source and the output device, and also offers an Advanced options button for performing stereo-to-mono conversion and for setting the recoding buffer size.

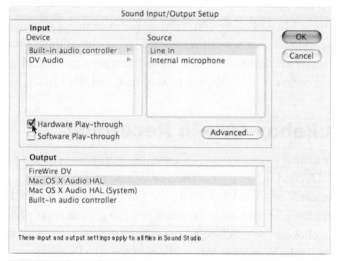

FIGURE 4.11 *Setting the sound input device (Built-in audio controller) and input source (Line In) for recording directly into a Macintosh using Sound Studio.*

Sound Studio lets you set the input volume levels precisely, and you can see the input levels as you record by choosing Window>Show Input Levels. You can adjust the volume separately for the left (L) and right (R) stereo channels. After setting the volume levels by playing the audio source device (or testing the microphones), click the Record button to record directly to disk, as shown in Figure 4.12.

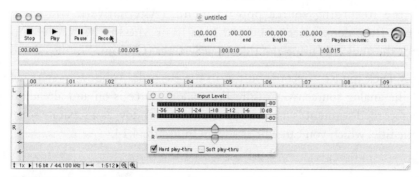

FIGURE 4.12 *Setting input levels and recording through the line-in connection using Sound Studio.*

Click the Stop button to stop recording, and save the audio file. You can use Sound Studio to edit the audio file, including fading in the sound at the beginning and fading it out at the end.

Sound Studio creates AIFF files, which you can then drag into iTunes and use for burning CDs. When you drag a song to your iTunes Library, a copy is made and placed inside the iTunes Music Folder. The original is not changed or moved. You can then convert the song to another format while leaving the original intact. For example, you might want to convert the AIFF files to another format, such as MP3 or AAC, as described earlier in this chapter, to save disk and iPod space.

MusicMatch Jukebox Line-In Recording

After connecting the analog source to your PC, use the appropriate control program for your sound card. Depending on your version of Windows, this may be a control panel specific to the card, or Windows Mixer, or the Sound and Audio Devices control panel. In Windows XP and other versions, you can get the appropriate control program by right-clicking the small speaker icon in your system tray, and choosing Adjust Audio Properties. In Windows Mixer, choose Options>Properties.

Find the settings for recording through microphone or line-in connection. In Windows Mixer, select Recording under Adjust volume, and turn on the option for Line-In or Microphone, to get to the Recording Control panel. The volume can then be set for recording either through the line-in connection or the microphone. In the Sound and Audio Devices control panel, click the Audio tab and then the Volume button in the Sound Recording section, as shown in Figure 4.13.

After setting the volume for recording, switch to (or open) MusicMatch Jukebox, choose Options>Settings and click the Recorder tab, and select Line In or Mic In from the Recording source pop-up menu. (Alternatively, you can choose Options>Recorder>Source and either Line In or Mic In.) MusicMatch Jukebox records the audio file using the Recorder Settings (Options>Settings>Recorder).

Finally, click the Rec (record) button in the Recorder window to start recording from the analog source. Make sure the analog source is on and already playing. Each recorded segment is listed in the Recorder window as a separate song with a generic title, which you can edit as shown in Figure 4.14.

FIGURE 4.13 *Setting the volume for recording through the microphone or line-in connection on a PC.*

FIGURE 4.14 *Recording directly into MusicMatch Jukebox through the microphone or line-in connection on a PC.*

MusicMatch Jukebox provides the Auto Song Detect option that can detect the end of a song from an analog source (such as a phonograph or tape player). To use it, choose Options>Settings>Recorder, and then click the Advanced button. Click the Active button to turn on Auto Song Detect. You can set the Gap Length, which is the amount of time between songs (typically about 1.5 seconds, or about 1500 ms.) that MusicMatch Jukebox uses to determine whether a song has ended and another begun. You can also set the Gap Level, which tells MusicMatch Jukebox to listen for a certain volume level to determine when a song is over (typically about 10% of the total volume or less).

Using the iTunes Equalizer

If the experts on high-fidelity sound agree on one thing, it is that there is no exact scientific definition of a high-fidelity system. The limitations of the human ear and variations in human taste, room acoustics, system distortions, and ambient noise all contribute to this fundamental inconsistency of opinion. As a result, most high-fidelity systems offer ways to customize the sound for your ears and your listening environment.

When you turn up the bass or treble on a stereo system, you are actually increasing the volume, or intensity, of certain frequencies while the music is playing. As you know, you aren't really changing the music itself, just the way it is playing back. As a discerning listener, you might change these bass and treble settings for each song.

With iTunes, you can change equalizer settings for one or more songs, and assign equalizer settings to songs so that they're used when you play back the songs on your iPod. (As of this writing, MusicMatch Jukebox does not offer this feature.)

The iTunes equalizer (EQ) lets you fine-tune specific sound frequencies in a more precise way than with bass and treble controls. You might pick entirely different equalizer settings for car speakers, home speakers, headphones, and other listening environments. You can adjust the frequencies directly, or use one of more than 20 built-in presets for various types of music from classical to rock. You can then assign the equalizer settings to a specific song or set of songs. With the equalizer settings, you can customize playback for different musical genres, listening environments, or speakers. You can even save your own presets.

To use the iTunes equalizer, click the equalizer button, which is on the bottom-right side of the iTunes window, just to the left of the visual effects and CD eject button, or choose Window>Equalizer.

The iTunes equalizer, shown in Figure 4.15, offers a Preamp control on the far left side. You can increase or decrease the volume in 3-decible increments up to 12 dB. Decibels are units that measure the intensity (or volume) of the frequencies. You can change the setting while playing the music so that you can hear the results right away.

Use the preamp volume to improve songs that were recorded too softly or too loudly. It adjusts the volume for all the frequencies together. If you want to make any adjustments to individual frequencies, you may want to adjust the preamp volume first if volume adjustment is needed, then move on to the specific frequencies.

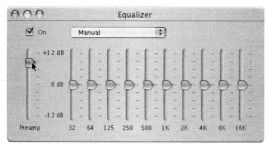

FIGURE 4.15   *Using the iTunes equalizer's Preamp slider to adjust volume across all frequencies.*

Adjusting Frequencies

The equalizer frequencies can be adjusted using sliders that look like mixing-board faders. The horizontal values across the equalizer represent part of the spectrum of human hearing. The deepest frequency (bass) is 32 hertz (Hz); the mid-range frequencies are 250 Hz and 500 Hz, and the higher frequencies go from 1 kHz (kilohertz) to 16 kHz (treble).

The vertical values on each bar represent decibels (dB), which measure the intensity of each frequency. Increase or decrease the frequencies in 3-decible increments by dragging the sliders up or down. You can adjust these settings while the music is playing and hear the effect immediately.

Using Equalizer Presets

iTunes offers presets, which are equalizer settings saved by name, so that you can quickly switch settings without having to make changes to each frequency slider. iTunes comes with more than 20 presets of the most commonly used equalizer settings, available for you in the pop-up menu, as shown in Figure 4.16.

Select one of the preset values from the pop-up menu while listening to music to hear its effect immediately.

You can also create your own presets. Choose Manual in the pop-up menu to make setting changes in the equalizer. Then choose Make Preset from the pop-up menu to save your changes, as shown in Figure 4.17. The name you use for the preset appears in the pop-up menu from that point on.

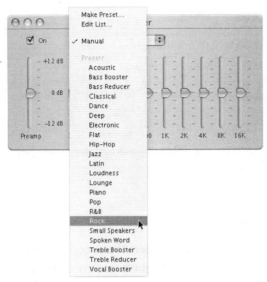

FIGURE 4.16   *Choosing one of the built-in equalizer presets in iTunes.*

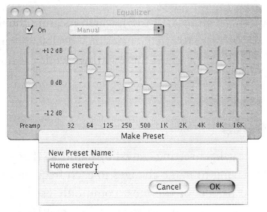

FIGURE 4.17   *Saving equalizer adjustments as a new custom preset in iTunes.*

Rename or delete the presets in your pop-up menu by choosing Edit List from the pop-up menu, which displays a window for renaming or deleting presets, as shown in Figure 4.18.

FIGURE 4.18   *Editing the equalizer preset pop-up list in iTunes.*

Assigning Presets to Songs

If you want to use different equalizer presets for different songs, especially presets for iPod playback, you can assign a preset in iTunes for each song that needs one. When you transfer the songs to your iPod, the preset stays assigned to it, and you can choose whether to use it when playing the song on your iPod.

You can assign any preset directly to a song in iTunes. To save your own unique equalizer settings with a song, you must first save those settings as a preset by choosing Make Preset from the pop-up menu and giving the preset a name, as shown in Figure 4.17. You can then assign your own preset to songs.

To assign a preset equalization to a song in iTunes:

1. Choose Edit>View Options. The View Options window appears, as shown in Figure 4.19, and you can select the columns to show in the song list.

2. Turn on the Equalizer option, and click OK.

   To turn on the Equalizer option, click the check box next to the column header, so that a check mark appears. An unchecked column header indicates a column that will not appear in the song list.

3. Locate a song in the list, and scroll the song list horizontally to see the Equalizer column.

4. Choose a preset from the pop-up menu in the Equalizer column.

The Equalizer column has a tiny pop-up menu, as shown in Figure 4.20, that lets you assign any preset to a song.

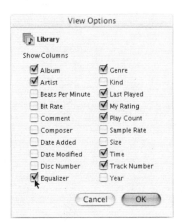

FIGURE 4.19 *Adding the Equalizer column to appear in the song list in iTunes.*

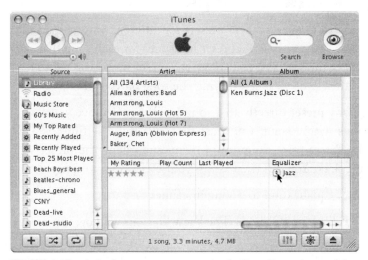

FIGURE 4.20 *Assigning a preset to a song in the Equalizer column of the song list in iTunes.*

Using Assigned Presets for Songs on Your iPod

The iPod's built-in equalizer modifies the volume of the frequencies of the sound for playback and offers a long list of presets to suit the type of music, or the type of environment. You can select an iPod equalizer preset by choosing Settings>EQ from the iPod's main menu, and selecting one of the presets.

The Off setting turns off the iPod's equalizer—no presets are used, not even one you may have assigned in iTunes. *You must choose an EQ setting to turn on the iPod's equalizer.*

However, if you have already assigned a preset to the song using iTunes, iPod uses the iTunes-assigned preset when you choose an EQ preset on the iPod. In other words, the assigned preset from iTunes takes precedence over the preset in the iPod. If you assign a preset to a song in iTunes, you can use it by turning on the iPod's equalizer—choose any EQ setting (other than Off), and the iPod uses the song's iTunes preset for playback. Unfortunately the iPod doesn't display the name of the iTunes preset (perhaps a future version will).

If you know in advance that certain songs should have specific presets assigned to them, use iTunes to assign the preset to the song before copying the song to the iPod. On the other hand, if you don't want your songs to be preordained to have a certain preset, and you want to experiment with the presets in the iPod to get better playback in different listening environments, *don't* assign a preset—wait until you have the song in your iPod, and then you can use the iPod's EQ presets.

You have now learned how to tweak the sounds for your iPod to your heart's content. The next chapter lets you manipulate data with your iPod in ways that other music players cannot.

Chapter 5

**Playing
Information**

Here's what you'll explore in this chapter:

- ◆ Using your iPod as a PDA
- ◆ Setting the time, date, alarm, and sleep timer
- ◆ Organizing calendars and contacts
- ◆ Updating the information on your iPod

Your iPod keeps time, and can even wake you up with your favorite music as an alarm. But your iPod can do a lot more. This chapter explains how to use the calendar function and keep your iPod's calendars synchronized with your computer's calendars. It also shows how you can put all your contact information—including addresses, phone numbers, email addresses, and comments—on your iPod for easy reference on the road.

Using Your iPod as a PDA

The iPod can help you manage your life almost as well as a fully featured PDA (personal digital assistant). You can use the iPod to view information you need when traveling, without the hassle of carrying a PDA along with your iPod and laptop computer.

If you like keyboards that are large enough to touch-type, you probably have trouble with the thumb-style keypads of PDAs. Small keyboards and clumsy human interfaces hamper the use of PDAs for input. I would rather use my laptop computer, which I carry with me when I travel, for all the input I would have to do with a PDA (such as contact information and calendar details). Laptops (and possibly the new tablet computers) are excellent for this purpose, and all my information is centralized on that machine.

Using the laptop for input, you never run the risk of being out-of-sync (as in accidentally overwriting the new content put into the PDA with the content from the laptop). As a result, you don't need a fully featured PDA. You can use the iPod alone if you want to view the information without changing it, and use your laptop to make changes.

Reading Books and Playing Games

There's a lot more to the iPod than just playing music. In particular, you can allevi-ate the boredom of travel by playing games, and "bookmark" your audio books from Audible.

Setting Bookmarks for Audible Books

When you use Audible books, articles, and spoken-word titles obtained from www.audible.com, you can automatically bookmark your place in the text with the iPod. Bookmarks work only with Audible files. If you have an audio book or spoken-word file in any other format, such as MP3, bookmarks are not available.

Use the Pause/Play button to pause an Audible file. Your iPod automatically book-marks that spot in the file. The next time you play that Audible file it starts playing from that spot.

Bookmarks are synchronized when you copy an Audible title to your iPod—whichever bookmark is further along in your iPod or your computer becomes the effective bookmark.

Playing Games

The games that come with the iPod—Brick, Parachute, and Solitaire—were added to alleviate boredom while traveling. You can play music while you play a game. To reach the games, choose Extras>Games.

Brick is similar to the original version of Pong—a ping–pong game against a wall. Parachute is a shooting gallery with helicopters that explode and paratroopers that drop down to kill you. However, by my own informal survey, the most popular game seems to be the Solitaire card game.

Putting Time on Your Side

The iPod keeps time for you. It has a digital clock that doubles as an alarm clock and a sleep timer. To view the clock, choose Extras>Clock from the main menu, as shown in Figures 5.1 and 5.2.

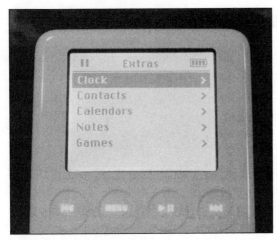

FIGURE 5.1 *Using your iPod's Extras menu to select the Clock.*

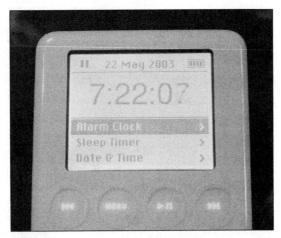

FIGURE 5.2 *Using the iPod's Clock menu.*

Setting the Clock and Sleep Timer

To set the date and time in your iPod, first press the Menu button to go back to the main menu, and then follow these steps:

1. Select Extras from the main menu, and then select Clock from the Extras menu (Extras>Clock).

2. Select the Date & Time option from the Clock menu.

3. Select Set Time Zone from the Date & Time menu.

4. Scroll the Time Zone list (which is in alphabetical order) and select a time zone.

5. The Date & Time menu appears again. Select the option to Set Date & Time.

6. The Date & Time display appears with up and down arrow indicators over the highlighted hours field. Use the scroll pad to change the hour in the Date & Time display: scroll clockwise to go forward in time, and counter-clockwise to go backward.

7. Click the center button after scrolling to the appropriate hour.

8. The up and down arrow indicators move to the next highlighted time field, minutes. Repeat Steps 6 and 7 for each field of the date and time: minutes, AM/PM, calendar date, calendar month, and year.

The Date & Time menu also offers the Time option that switches time display from "12-hour" to "24-hour" (military style). You can also select the Time in Title option in this menu, and click the center button to switch it from "Off" to "On" to show the time in the menu title of your iPod's menus.

Just like a travel clock radio, you can use your iPod to play music for a while before going to sleep (a sleep timer). To set the sleep timer, select Sleep Timer from the Clock menu, and it shows a list of durations, from 15 minutes to 120 minutes, in 15-minute intervals. You can select a duration, or "Off" (at the top of the list) to turn off the sleep timer. Start a playlist, and your iPod will shut itself off and go to sleep according to the duration you set.

Setting the Alarm

From the iPod's Clock menu, you can choose Alarm Clock, as shown in Figures 5.2 and 5.3, and set the time of the alarm and the playlist to start playing as the alarm sound (the playlist "On-The-Go" is set in Figure 5.3). You can use whatever playlist you want. The playlist plays until you stop it.

To set the Alarm Clock, follow these steps:

1. From the main menu, choose Extras>Clock>Alarm Clock.

2. Scroll to Alarm in the Alarm Clock menu, and click the center button so that "Off" changes to "On."

3. Choose Time in the Alarm Clock menu.

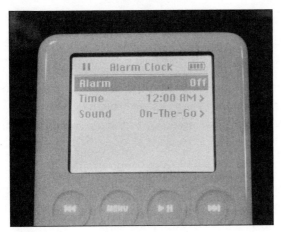

FIGURE 5.3 *Using the iPod's Alarm menu.*

4. The Alarm Time display appears with up and down arrow indicators. Use the scroll pad to change the time in the Alarm Time display: scroll clockwise to go forward in time, and counterclockwise to go backward.

5. Click the center button after scrolling to the appropriate alarm time.

6. In the Alarm Clock menu that appears again, choose the Sound option.

7. Select a playlist, or "Beep" (at the top of the list), as your alarm sound.

When the alarm goes off, the playlist plays until you stop it by pressing the Play/Pause button.

Organizing Calendars

A calendar can be useful while traveling, especially one that has the information you need for appointments and scheduling. You can put the location of events into a calendar and keep track of day-to-day appointments and meetings, with details on each appointment. You can also maintain a "to-do" list of projects and tasks. You input all this information on your computer, and then transfer it to your iPod for use while traveling.

You can view your iPod's calendar by choosing Extras>Calendars>All. But this function is far more useful after you've updated your iPod with your calendars and to-do lists created on your computer.

Using iCal (Macintosh)

iCal, the free desktop calendar application from Apple, which you can download from the Apple site (at http://www.apple.com/software/), creates calendars and "to-do" lists that you can copy to your iPod. You can create calendars for different activities, such as home, office, road tours, exercise/diet schedules, mileage logs, and so on, and view them separately or all together. After editing your calendars and "to-do" lists on the Mac, you can synchronize your iPod to have the same information.

To create an event in your iCal calendar, open iCal, which displays a calendar as shown in Figure 5.4 (in its monthly view). Choose File>New Event to add an event to a particular day.

FIGURE 5.4   *Using iCal on the Mac to add a new event to a calendar.*

The Event Info window appears, as shown in Figure 5.5, and you can type a name for the event, change the date and time for the event, and add a description. You can turn on the "All-day event" option to make the time of day irrelevant. You can also assign a status to the Status pop-up menu (with the values Tentative, Confirmed, Cancelled, or None), and assign the event to a specific calendar, since you can have multiple calendars.

FIGURE 5.5   *Changing the event information*
                 for an event in iCal for the Mac.

To see the Event Info window for any event and make further changes, select the event and choose Window>Inspector.

You can maintain multiple calendars in iCal, and view all of them at the same time or separately in either iCal or on the iPod. To create a new calendar, click the plus (+) button (or choose File>New Calendar) and give the calendar a name, as shown in Figure 5.6.

iCal can keep track of your "to-do" list, and your list is automatically copied to your iPod along with your calendars. Choose File>New To Do to add an item to the list.

You can also use iCal to import calendars from other applications that support the iCal or vCal format. The iPod supports industry-standard iCalendar and vCalendar files, which can be exported by many applications including Microsoft Entourage, Microsoft Outlook, and Palm Desktop, and you can import iCalendar files into iCal to merge them with your iCal calendars. Choose File>Import and locate the calendar file, which should have the ".ics" extension. To use vCalendar files exported from another application, first read about using your iPod as a disk drive in Chapter 6.

With your calendar and "to-do" information in iCal, you can automatically transfer your calendars and your "to-do" list to your iPod using iSync. See "Updating Information on Your iPod" later in this chapter.

FIGURE 5.6   *Adding another new calendar in iCal to manage multiple calendars on a single iPod.*

Using Microsoft Outlook (Windows)

Microsoft Outlook, provided with Windows, provides extensive calendar and scheduling functions and task management. You need only a fraction of Outlook's features to keep a calendar and to-do list that can be viewed on your iPod. Many of the more advanced functions, such as scheduling conferences and meetings to coincide with the schedules of other people on a network, have no meaning on an iPod. Nevertheless, the iPod is useful for viewing the results of Outlook activity. If you use those features, any event, appointment, or meeting that displays in your Outlook calendar is also copied to your iPod along with the calendar.

You can click on any time slot in the Outlook calendar, as shown in Figure 5.7, to type an appointment, event, or any other calendar item. To create an appointment with start and end times and a location, as shown in Figure 5.8, select a block of time and right-click to choose New Appointment (or New Recurring Appointment for appointments that repeat often). You can also select a block of time and choose File>New>Appointment.

FIGURE 5.7 *Selecting a time slot in the Outlook calendar for an appointment.*

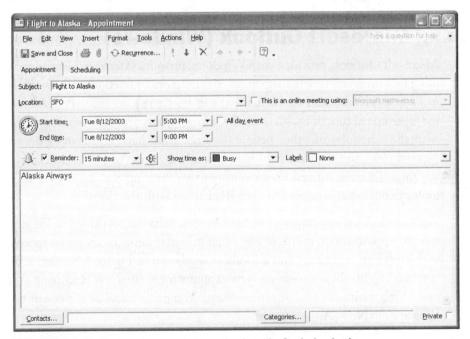

FIGURE 5.8 *Typing appointment information into the Outlook calendar.*

To create a "to-do" task in Outlook, choose New>Task, and type a subject name for the task. To make the task a recurring task, click the Recurrence option and choose a frequency (Daily, Weekly, Monthly, or Yearly) for the recurring task. Finally, click Save and Close to save the task.

With your calendar and "to-do" information established in Outlook, you can export the calendars and "to-do" list to your iPod. See "Updating Information on Your iPod," later in this chapter.

Organizing Contacts

You may be using a cell phone to keep phone numbers handy, but you can't store all your other contact information that might be useful while traveling, such as email addresses and comments. The iPod can store up to a thousand contacts right alongside your music.

If you use an email program such as Mail with Address Book on the Macintosh or Microsoft Outlook on a Windows-based PC, you already have an address book, though it may have only names and email addresses in it at this time. You can add more information to each person's "card" in either Address Book (Mac) or Microsoft Outlook (Windows). If you use some other email program, chances are your email addresses are already stored in the appropriate "vCard" format or your email program lets you export them as vCards, which work on your iPod.

Using Address Book (Macintosh)

Every Mac comes with the Mail and Address Book applications that work together to help you maintain your email contacts. All you need to do is use Address Book to add more information, such as physical addresses, phone numbers, and comments, to each person's card in the address book as you wish. With Address Book, keeping your iPod synchronized with your newest addresses and phone numbers is simple and automatic.

You can add new people to your address book from the Mail program by selecting an email message and choosing Message>Add Sender to Address Book. You can then open Address Book, click on a name in the Name column, as shown in Figure 5.9, and click the Edit button to edit the person's card, as shown in Figure 5.10.

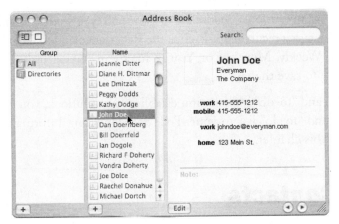

FIGURE 5.9 *Selecting a name in Address Book on a Mac to edit or add personal contact information.*

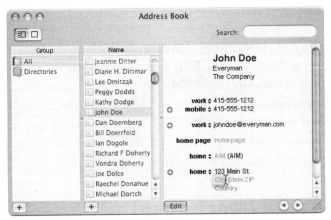

FIGURE 5.10 *After clicking the Edit button, you can edit the personal contact information for a name in Address Book on a Mac.*

When editing a person's card in Address Book, you can jump from field to field by pressing the Tab key. If some of the fields don't apply, you can skip them and they won't be shown in the final card for that person. You can enter a two-line address by pressing Return to continue to the second line. To add more fields, such as additional phone numbers, click the plus (+) button next to a field name. When you are finished editing information, click the Edit button to save your changes.

To add a new card for a person, choose File>New Card, or click the plus (+) button at the bottom of the Name column. You can also drag a vCard-formatted address from an email message directly into Address Book to create a new card.

With your contact information in Address Book, you can automatically transfer the contact list to your iPod using iSync. See "Updating Information on Your iPod," later in this chapter.

Using Microsoft Outlook (Windows and Mac)

Microsoft Outlook, provided with Windows and also available on the Mac, provides extensive features for managing contacts with email and address information. You can also import into Outlook address books and contact information from programs such as Eudora, Lotus Organizer, Netscape Messenger, Microsoft Mail, or Microsoft Schedule+.

The Address Book in Outlook lets you gather address books from other sources, including Microsoft Exchange Server and Internet directory services (depending on how you've set up Outlook). It also includes all the contacts in your Outlook Contacts folder. When you update information in your Contacts folder, the Outlook Address Book is updated as well, so you can make all your changes in the Contacts folder.

To create a contact in Outlook, choose New>Contact, and type a name for the contact, as shown in Figure 5.11 (Windows version). To enter multiple entries for a field, such as more than one physical address or email address, click the down-arrow next to the field to display more entries for that field. Enter all the information you want (or as little as you want). When finished, click Save and Close to save the contact. Your contacts are displayed in the Contacts window of Outlook, as shown in Figure 5.12.

You can also create a new contact automatically for the sender of an email message you receive. Open the email message, and in the From field, right-click the name you want to add to your Contacts folder, and choose Add to Contacts.

With your contact information in the Contacts folder in Outlook, you can export contacts in the vCard format to your iPod, as discussed in the following sections.

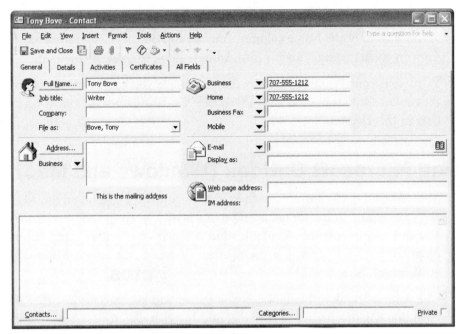

FIGURE 5.11 *Typing contact information into Outlook.*

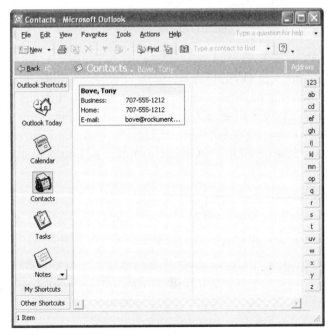

FIGURE 5.12 *Displaying contacts in Outlook.*

Updating Information on Your iPod

As you make changes to addresses, phone numbers, calendar events, and to-do lists, you will want to copy that information to your iPod. You can do this as often as you like. When you take your iPod on the road, the information is in the palm of your hand.

On the Mac, the iSync application can keep your iPod updated automatically, and you can also update manually by using the iPod as a hard disk, as described in Chapter 6. iSync is available for downloading free from Apple (http://www.apple.com/software/).

On a PC running Windows, you can enable your iPod to operate in disk mode, and copy files (or export directly) to the iPod just like an external disk drive.

Synchronizing with iSync (Macintosh)

To install iSync, download it from the Apple site (www.apple.com) and follow the instructions that appear for each step of the installation. At the end, your copy of iSync should be located in your Applications folder.

After installing iSync, connect your iPod to your Mac, open iSync, and choose Devices>Add Device. iSync searches for all your devices, and lets you select which ones to use with iSync, including your iPod, which appears with the name you assigned to it. Select the iPod, and it appears in the iSync bar, as shown in Figure 5.13.

FIGURE 5.13 *Selecting one of two named iPods ("Mojo iPod" and "Bobbie_McGee") for synchronization with iSync on the Mac.*

After adding the device, iSync keeps the icon in the iSync bar, so that each time you run iSync, you can click the icon and the device's synchronization settings appear. You can keep track of multiple iPods with iSync, as shown in Figure 5.13 (with iPods named "Mojo iPod" and "Bobby_McGee").

The settings for synchronizing your iPod, shown in Figure 5.14, include synchronizing all contacts and calendars, or just the ones you select. You can turn on the "Automatically synchronize when iPod is connected" option, so that every time you connect your iPod, iSync goes to work. If you don't want that level of automation, you can launch iSync anytime and click the Sync Now button.

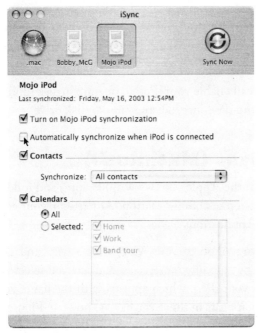

FIGURE 5.14 *Using the iSync synchronization settings for the selected iPod.*

iSync performs the synchronization, pausing to inform you that you are about to change your iPod's calendars, as shown in Figure 5.15.

After finishing with iSync, be sure to drag your iPod to the trash before disconnecting it. You can also use the Eject iPod button in iTunes (which replaces the CD eject button when you select the iPod in the Source list).

To copy calendars, contacts, and other information from your Mac to your iPod manually, read Chapter 6.

FIGURE 5.15 *The iSync safeguard warns you before synchronizing calendars from iCal with your iPod.*

Copying Calendars and Contacts to Your iPod (Windows)

To update your iPod from a Windows PC, you must first enable the iPod's disk mode, and then browse the iPod in Windows just like any other disk drive. You can then copy contacts and calendar files directly to the iPod folders that use them.

Enabling Disk Mode

To enable disk mode for the iPod, follow these steps:

1. Connect your iPod to your PC, and wait for it to be recognized by MusicMatch Jukebox. Your iPod should appear in the PortablesPlus window under the Attached Portable Devices folder. If the window is not yet open, choose File>Send to Portable Device.

2. Select the iPod, and click the Options button, then the iPod tab, and choose the Enable disk mode option, as shown in Figure 5.16.

3. Click OK to close the Options window.

Choose My Computer, and your iPod should appear just like any other removable disk in the My Computer window under "Devices with Removable Storage," as shown in Figure 5.17. On my Windows PC, my iPod appeared assigned to drive E (see Figure 5.17); on your system, the drive assignment will vary according to the devices you already connected to your PC.

Double-click the iPod icon in the My Computer window to open the iPod as a disk and see its folders, as shown in Figure 5.18. The iPod is supplied with the Calendars, Contacts, and Notes folders.

FIGURE 5.16 *Enabling disk mode for the iPod in Windows.*

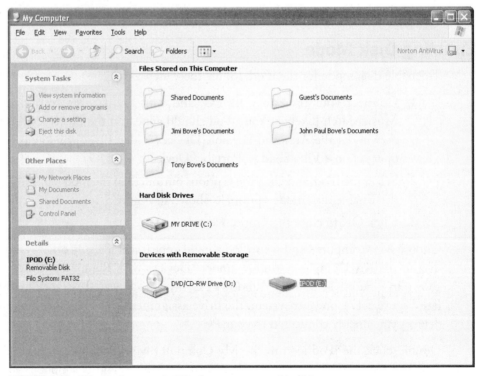

FIGURE 5.17 *The iPod appears in Windows as a removable disk.*

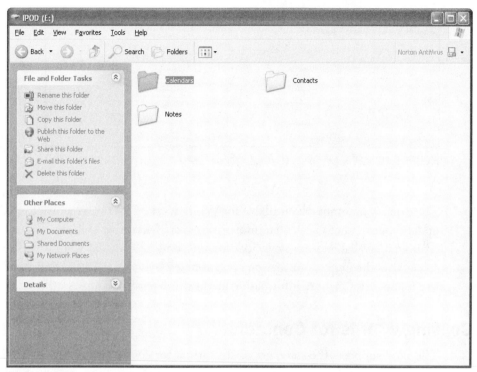

FIGURE 5.18 *Opening the iPod as a disk to see its folders.*

Copying Calendar Files

The iPod supports industry-standard iCalendar and vCalendar files, which can be exported by many applications. You can copy these files directly to your iPod's Calendars folder by opening the Calendars folder and dragging files into it from another folder. Figure 5.19 shows the iCalendar-formatted calendar files "Work," "Home," and "Band tour" in the Calendars folder of the iPod.

To save calendar information in the iCalendar format from Outlook, you must save each appointment separately as an ".ics" file. To use these files with the iPod, so that the appointments are displayed in the iPod's calendar, the ".ics" files must be stored in your iPod's Calendars folder. Select the appointment in the calendar view, or open the appointment by double-clicking it. Use the Save As command, and choose iCalendar from the "Save as type" pop-up menu, then choose a destination for the ".ics" (iCalendar) file. The destination can be a folder on your hard disk, or it can be the iPod's Calendars folder. If you choose a folder on your hard disk, be sure to copy the files to the iPod's Calendars folder.

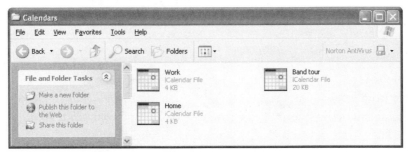

FIGURE 5.19 *Calendars in the iCalendar format are stored in your iPod's Calendars folder.*

Third-party programs are available for Windows iPod users that will automatically update your iPod with calendar information from Microsoft Outlook. For example, iPodSync, available from www.ipodlounge.com, keeps your Microsoft Outlook calendar and contact information synchronized between your PC and your iPod. See Chapter 6 for more information about third-party Windows utilities.

Copying vCards for Contacts

The iPod supports the standard vCard format for contact information. Microsoft Outlook and other programs can export vCard files for contacts, which you can then copy to the Contacts folder on your iPod. Alternatively, you can export vCard files directly to the Contacts folder from the program.

To export a vCard from Microsoft Outlook, open the contact in the Outlook Contacts folder and choose File>Export to vCard File. Type the filename for the vCard file and a choose a destination folder. You can use your hard disk as a destination and then copy the file to the Contacts folder on your iPod, or you can locate the Contacts folder and save to it directly.

Figure 5.20 shows the vCard-formatted contact files "address_export," "ipod_created_instructions," and "ipod_created_sample" in the Contacts folder of the iPod. The latter two are supplied with the iPod to show a sample contact and to provide instructions you can read on the iPod display. The "address_export" file is a vCard file.

Microsoft Outlook exports a single vCard file per contact. You can copy single or multiple vCard files into the Contacts folder. The iPod can manage up to 1000 contacts, which can be any combination of single or multiple-contact vCard files. Other programs, such as Lotus Notes, can also export vCard files. Select the contacts you want to export, choose File>Export, and choose vCard 3.0 in the "Save as type" pop-up menu before clicking Export.

Third-party programs are available for Windows iPod users that will automatically update your iPod with contacts from Microsoft Outlook. For example, iPodSync, available from www.ipodlounge.com, keeps your Microsoft Outlook calendar and contact information synchronized between your PC and your iPod. See Chapter 6 for more information about third-party Windows utilities.

FIGURE 5.20 *Contacts in the vCard format are stored in the iPod's Contacts folder.*

Using Calendars on Your iPod

On your iPod, you can view a single calendar or all your calendars by choosing Extras>Calendar. You can then use the scroll pad to scroll through the list of calendars to select one, or you can select All to view all the calendars at once, merged into one.

After selecting a calendar or All (scrolling to highlight it and pressing the center button), use the scroll pad to scroll through the days of the calendar. Press the center button to select a day. Then scroll through the day's list of events or appoint-ments, and press the center button on a highlighted item to see details.

Press the Next/Fast-Forward or Previous/Rewind buttons to skip to the next or previous month. To see your to-do list, choose Extras>Calendar>To Do, and scroll through the list of tasks to select one and view its details.

Using Contacts on Your iPod

You can view the contacts in your iPod by choosing Extras>Contacts, using the scroll pad to highlight a name, and pressing the center button to select a name and display the contact information.

The iPod's contact list is sorted automatically, and the iPod displays contact names in alphabetical order, according to last name by default. You can choose whether to display contact names by last name first or first name first. Choose Settings>Contacts>Display. Then press the center button in the scroll pad for each option:

◆ **First Last:** Displays the contact list first name first, and then last name last, as in "John Lennon."

◆ **Last, First:** Displays the contact list last name first, followed by a comma and first name, as in "Lennon, John."

You can also change the way contacts are sorted. The sort operation uses the entire name, but you decide whether to use the first name first or the last name first. Choose Settings>Contacts>Sort. Then press the center button in the scroll pad for each option:

◆ **First Last:** Sorts the contact list by first name, followed by the last name, so that "George Harrison" sorts under "George" (after George Duke but before George Michael).

◆ **Last, First:** Sorts the contacts by last name, followed by the first name, so that "Arlo Guthrie" sorts under "Guthrie" ("Guthrie, Arlo" appears after "Grisman, David" but before "Guthrie, Woody").

Your iPod is now a lot more useful. You can look up contacts, keep track of calendar events and to-do items, and use it as an alarm clock with music. The next chapter describes how you can also use your iPod to keep a safe backup of your most important files, and even help restore your computer to life if your operating system won't work.

Chapter 6

Using Advanced Features

Here's what you'll explore in this chapter:

- Using your iPod as a hard disk to copy personal information and files
- Customizing your iPod settings and main menu
- Using your iPod as a Mac startup disk
- Converting your iPod from Mac to Windows or from Windows to Mac
- Discovering third-party utilities that help you work with your iPod

This chapter describes how to get the most out of your iPod investment using advanced functions and third-party software. You learn how to customize the iPod menu, and how to use your iPod as an external and portable hard disk, holding files you can transfer to other computers or keep as a secure backup while on the road. (Try *that* with your PDA.)

This chapter also covers installing a Mac system on an iPod in order to boot your computer from the iPod—a useful technique for troubleshooting your internal Mac system and fixing your internal hard disk.

If you are a Mac user and you want to convert the iPod over to Windows use, this chapter explains how to do it, and also how to convert the iPod from Windows to Mac. In addition, this chapter describes some of the popular third-party applications and utilities that add functionality to the Windows and Mac versions of the iPod.

Using Your iPod as a Macintosh Disk

The iPod, as shipped, is formatted as a Macintosh disk and can be connected to any Mac. And like any hard disk, you can transfer files and applications from your computer to your iPod and take them with you wherever you go. The iPod is smart enough to keep your files separate from your music collection so that they will not be accidentally erased when you update your music.

Mounting the iPod as a Disk

To use your iPod as a hard disk on a Mac, follow these steps:

1. Connect your iPod to your Mac and open iTunes. To prevent iPod from automatically updating itself, hold down the Command and Option keys.

2. Select the iPod name in the iTunes Source list.

3. Click the iPod Options button to open the iPod Preferences window.

4. Turn on the Enable FireWire Disk Use option, as shown in Figure 6.1, and click OK to close the window.

FIGURE 6.1   *Turning on the Enable FireWire Disk Use option to use your iPod as a disk on a Mac.*

You can now open the iPod icon in the Finder to see its contents, just like any disk mounted on your Mac desktop.

The iPod hard disk opens up to show three folders: Calendars, Contacts, and Notes, as shown in Figure 6.2. You can add new folders, rename your custom folders, and generally use the iPod as a hard disk, but don't rename these three folders because they link directly to the Calendar, Contacts, and Notes functions on your iPod.

 TIP

To see how much free disk space is left on your iPod, you can use the Finder. Select the iPod icon on the Finder desktop, and choose File>Show Info.

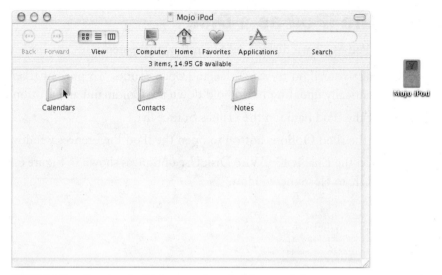

FIGURE 6.2 *Opening the iPod mounted on the Mac as a disk.*

Copying Calendars and Contacts Manually

With your iPod mounted as a disk, you can copy files and folders to it, including calendar and contact files. You may want to copy these files manually rather than using iSync, as described in Chapter 5, because iSync takes longer to synchronize contact information than it takes to copy new contacts over to the iPod in the Finder.

A vCard, or *virtual card*, is a standard method of exchanging contact information. The iPod sorts and displays up to a thousand contacts in the vCard format. The iPod is compatible with popular Mac applications such as Microsoft Entourage, Microsoft Outlook, and Palm Desktop, as well as Address Book. You can use any of these programs to export your contacts as vCards directly into the Contacts folder of your iPod. In most cases, you can simply drag vCard-formatted contacts from the application's address book to your iPod's Contacts folder.

If you use Address Book and you don't want to use iSync, or if you use any other application that exports vCards, you can export one card, or a group of cards, or even the entire list, as a vCard file (with a ".vcf" extension). Then drag the vCard file or multiple vCard files into the Contacts folder, as shown in Figure 6.3. Contacts must be in the vCard format to use with the iPod.

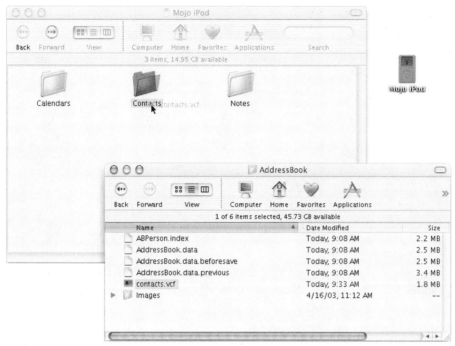

FIGURE 6.3   *Adding a vCard file of addresses and phone numbers to the Contacts folder on your iPod.*

As of this writing, the iPod supports only a portion of what you can put into a vCard. For example, you can include photos and sounds in vCards used by other applications, but you can't open up those portions of the vCard using the iPod.

iPod supports industry-standard iCalendar and vCalendar files, which can be exported by many applications including Microsoft Entourage, Microsoft Outlook, and Palm Desktop. In most cases, you can drag an iCalendar file (with the filename extension ".ics") or a vCalendar file (with the filename extension ".vcs") to your iPod Calendars folder, as shown in Figure 6.4.

Managing Files and Folders

You can add new folders, rename your custom folders, and generally use the iPod as a hard disk. To keep data organized, you can create new folders on your iPod, as shown in Figure 6.5, and then drag files and folders to the newly created folders.

To delete files and folders from your iPod, drag them to the trashcan just as you would with any external hard disk.

FIGURE 6.4 *Adding exported calendars in the iCalendar format to the Calendars folder on your iPod.*

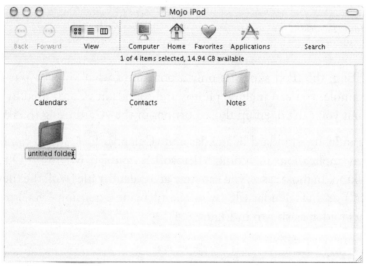

FIGURE 6.5 *Creating a new folder on the iPod.*

WARNING

Do not use a disk utility program, such as Disk Utility or Drive Setup, to erase the iPod. If you erase the iPod disk this way, it may be unable to play music.

Un-Mounting the iPod

When you are finished copying files to or from your iPod, un-mount the iPod by dragging its icon to the trash. As an alternative, you can click the iPod Eject button that appears in the bottom-right side of the iTunes window, replacing the CD eject button.

After un-mounting, your iPod displays the message, "OK to disconnect." You can then disconnect your iPod from its dock, or disconnect the dock from the computer.

 WARNING

Never disconnect an iPod before un-mounting it. If you do, you may have to reset your iPod as described in "Resetting Your iPod" in Chapter 7.

Putting the Mac System on Your iPod

You can turn your iPod into a Macintosh system disk, which can be useful in times of crisis. Apple doesn't officially support this procedure, but you can load the iPod with system software and use the iPod to start up your Mac.

Why is this useful? If any portion of your usual startup disk is damaged, your system may not start properly. When this happens, you ordinarily use the installation CDs to start the computer, scan and fix the hard-disk trouble spots, and reinstall the system. However, if you are on the road with a malfunctioning Mac but without your system installation CDs, and you need to access your Mac, you can at least start the computer with your iPod. You can then scan and fix the hard-disk trouble spots, and also use any other files or applications you previously put on your iPod.

For example, you may want to take an important document on the road, to use with TextEdit. You can copy the document, TextEdit, and a custom version of Mac OS X to your iPod for emergency use. If your PowerBook fails, you can start the PowerBook from your iPod, and run TextEdit from the iPod, using the iPod as a hard disk.

To copy files and applications to the iPod, mount the iPod as a disk, as described earlier in this chapter. To install a custom version of OS X on your iPod, follow these steps:

1. Insert your Mac OS X installation CD into your Mac, and restart the Mac with the installation CD while holding down the C key to start the computer from the CD.

2. Follow the directions to start up the installation process.

3. When you are asked to select a destination, choose the iPod. Do *not* use the option to erase and format the hard disk, because the iPod can't be erased and formatted this way.

4. Specify a custom installation rather than a standard installation, so that you don't use up too much iPod disk space.

5. In the custom installation section, choose only the languages you need. These language options take up a lot of space and you probably won't need them in emergencies.

6. After installation finishes and the computer restarts from the iPod, continue through the setup procedure, and then use Software Update in System Preferences to update the system on your iPod with the updates released after the date of your installation CDs.

Now, if your Mac does not start up properly, connect your iPod with its backup Mac system to your Mac. As the only other hard disk connected with a system installed, the iPod should start up your Mac with its minimal system. You can then use the Mac Finder to copy files to and from your iPod and any other working hard disks on the Mac.

Using Your iPod as a Windows Disk

The iPod, as shipped, is formatted as a Macintosh disk. However, when you connect it to a Windows-based PC and run the supplied installation software, the iPod is transformed into a Windows-formatted disk. From that point on it can be used only with Windows PCs, unless you convert it back to the Mac format as described in "Switching from Windows to Mac," later in this chapter.

Like any hard disk, you can transfer files and applications from your computer to your iPod and take them with you wherever you go. The iPod is smart enough to keep your files separate from your music collection so that they will not be accidentally erased when you update your music.

Mounting the iPod as a Disk (Windows)

You can enable the iPod's disk mode in Windows using either MusicMatch Jukebox or the iPod Manager utility. In MusicMatch Jukebox, follow these steps:

1. Connect your iPod to your PC, and wait for it to be recognized by MusicMatch Jukebox. Your iPod should appear in the PortablesPlus window under the Attached Portable Devices folder. If the window is not yet open, choose File>Send to Portable Device.

2. Select the iPod, and click the Options button, then the iPod tab, and choose the Enable disk mode option.

3. Click OK to close the Options window.

The iPod Manager utility, shown in Figure 6.6, is provided with iPod for Windows to change iPod settings, launch the software updater, check the Apple site for updates, and change the home application for the iPod (set to MusicMatch Jukebox by default). To enable disk mode with iPod Manager, follow these steps:

1. Connect your iPod to the PC running Windows.

2. Click on the iPod Watcher in the system tray (or right-click the icon and choose iPod Manager from the pop-up menu), or open iPod Manager directly by choosing Start Menu>All Programs>iPod>iPod Manager.

3. Turn on the Enable disk mode option, as shown in Figure 6.6.

4. Click OK to close the iPod Manager window.

 TIP

To see how much free space is left on your iPod, you can use iPod Manager, which shows you the total amount of storage space on your iPod and the amount already used.

You can now open your iPod in the My Computer window to see its contents, just like any storage device connected to your Windows computer. The iPod is assigned a drive letter, such as "E" (depending on how many devices you already have connected to the PC).

FIGURE 6.6 *Using iPod Manager to enable disk mode.*

The iPod disk opens up to show three folders: Calendars, Contacts, and Notes, as described in Chapter 5, "Copying Calendars and Contacts to Your iPod (Windows)." You can add new folders, rename your custom folders, and generally use the iPod as a hard disk, but don't rename these three folders, because they link directly to the Calendar, Contacts, and Notes functions on your iPod.

Managing Files and Folders

To keep data organized, you can create new folders on your iPod, as shown in Figure 6.7, and then copy files and folders to the newly created folders.

To delete files and folders from your iPod, select the file or folder and choose File>Delete (or choose Delete from the File and Folder Tasks menu) as you would with a file or folder on any other disk.

 WARNING

Do not use a disk utility program to erase the iPod. If you erase the iPod disk this way, it may be unable to play music.

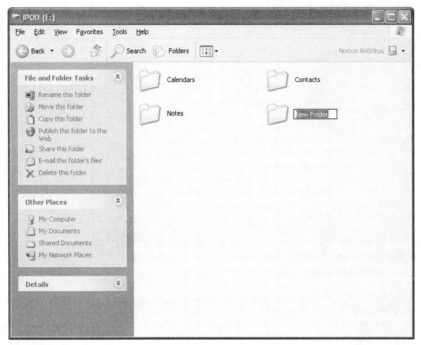

FIGURE 6.7 *Creating a new folder on the iPod.*

You can also use applications to export files directly to your iPod. For example, in Outlook, you can export a vCard file for a contact directly into your iPod's Contacts folder, as shown in Figures 6.8 and 6.9. After choosing File>Export to vCard, as described in Chapter 5, "Copying Calendars and Contacts to Your iPod (Windows)," use the Save in drop-down menu in the dialog box to choose the iPod as a disk, then choose the Contacts folder.

Un-Mounting (Ejecting) the iPod

When you are finished copying files to or from your iPod, un-mount the iPod (eject it). You can choose one of three ways to do this:

◆ Click the Eject button in MusicMatch Jukebox

◆ Use the iPod Watcher in the system tray

◆ Use the Safe Remove Hardware icon in the system tray

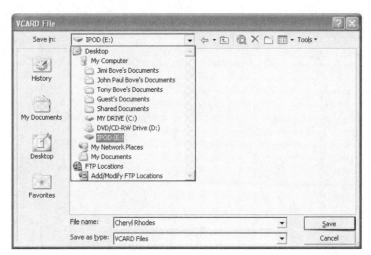

FIGURE 6.8 *Choosing the iPod as the destination disk to save an exported vCard file.*

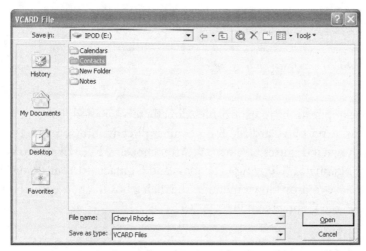

FIGURE 6.9 *Choosing the Contacts folder on the iPod to save the exported vCard file.*

 WARNING

There is one method you should never use to un-mount your iPod: Never use the contextual menu—the menu that pops up if you right-click the iPod icon in the My Computer window—and its Eject option. This Eject option does not work with the iPod and may damage files on the iPod.

To un-mount your iPod from within MusicMatch Jukebox, follow these steps:

1. Close any application other than MusicMatch Jukebox (such as iPod Manager) that is using the iPod.

2. Select iPod in the MusicMatch Jukebox PortablesPlus window.

3. Click the Eject button in the lower-left corner of the MusicMatch Jukebox PortablesPlus window.

4. An alert box appears. Click Yes.

5. It takes about 15 seconds before the iPod is ready to be disconnected. The PortablesPlus window displays the message, "Ejecting iPod. Please wait..." until it finishes, and then it displays, "It is now safe to disconnect iPod."

6. Wait until the iPod displays "OK to disconnect" and then disconnect your iPod from the computer.

Follow these steps to un-mount your iPod using the Safely Remove Hardware icon in the Windows system tray:

1. Close any applications (such as MusicMatch Jukebox and iPod Manager) that are still using the iPod.

2. At the bottom-right of the screen, click the Safely Remove Hardware icon.

3. Select the Apple IEEE 1394 (FireWire) device if you are using FireWire, or the USB Mass Storage device if you're using USB, from the pop-up menu.

4. An alert box appears. Click OK.

5. Wait until the iPod displays "OK to disconnect" and then disconnect your iPod from the computer.

Follow these steps to un-mount your iPod using the iPod Watcher icon in the Windows system tray:

1. Close any applications (such as MusicMatch Jukebox) that are still using the iPod.

2. At the bottom-right of the screen, right-click the iPod Watcher icon.

3. Choose Unmount from the pop-up menu.

4. An alert box appears. Click OK.

5. Wait until the iPod displays "OK to disconnect" and then disconnect your iPod from the computer.

WARNING

Never disconnect an iPod before un-mounting it. If you do, you may have to reset your iPod, as described in "Resetting Your iPod," in Chapter 7.

Switching from Mac to Windows

The iPod is specially configured with software for either a Mac or a Windows-based PC. The iPod is initially formatted in the HFS Plus file format, which is optimized for performance and usability in Mac OS X and 9. The iPod for Windows software reformats the iPod to the FAT32 file format, which is optimized for performance and usability in Windows Me, 2000, and XP. Note that once it is reformatted, it will only work with Windows unless you reformat it for Macs.

Switching from Mac to Windows reformats the iPod's disk, wiping out all your music and data, and restores the iPod to its factory default settings, removing any custom settings. After reformatting, you have to update your iPod with music and information, and customize your settings again.

When you connect a Mac-formatted iPod to a Windows PC, the PC doesn't recognize it, even if you are using an appropriate FireWire or USB connection, because Windows doesn't support the HFS Plus file format.

You need the iPod for Windows CD-ROM that came with your iPod (if you bought the Mac version, you may need to purchase this from Apple).

 WARNING

When installing the iPod for Windows, be sure your iPod is disconnected from the PC before starting the installation procedure.

To install the proper software to make your iPod work with Windows, and to reformat the disk for Windows, follow these steps *before* connecting your iPod to your PC:

1. Insert the iPod for Windows CD-ROM into your Windows-based PC. Do not connect your iPod to your PC yet.

2. If the installer doesn't open automatically, double-click the CD-ROM icon in the My Computer window, and then double-click the Setup icon.

3. Click Install, and follow the instructions as they appear. iPod for Windows software must be installed on the C: drive in order to work.

4. The installation instructions will tell you when it is time to connect your iPod to the PC. Go ahead and connect it to the PC, and follow the instructions to continue installation until installation is finished; then skip to Step 7. If the PC doesn't recognize the iPod, continue with the following steps.

5. Open the iPod Updater by choosing Start>Programs>iPod>Updater.

6. Click the Restore button, and follow the directions that appear. The restore operation resets the iPod to its factory default settings and reformats the iPod disk.

7. Continue with the iPod for Windows installation, following the instructions that appear, as described in Chapter 1.

After following these steps, the iPod's hard disk has been formatted in the FAT32 format and will work with computers that have a compatible version of the Windows operating system.

 TIP

To see if your iPod is formatted correctly, choose Settings>About from the iPod main menu, and use the scroll pad to scroll down past the serial number. If the disk is formatted for Macintosh, the serial number or model number is the last item in the About screen. If the disk is formatted for Windows, the last item on the screen is: "Format: Windows."

You can transfer your iTunes music library to MusicMatch Jukebox, but MusicMatch Jukebox supports only music in the MP3 and WAV formats. All other music files must be converted to these formats for use with MusicMatch Jukebox. (You can't convert copyright-protected music purchased from the iTunes Music Store.) Once your music is in the MusicMatch Jukebox library, you can update your iPod automatically, as described in Chapter 1.

To transfer your music library from iTunes to MusicMatch Jukebox, follow these steps:

1. Consolidate your iTunes music library on your Mac (as described in "iTunes Library Backup and Sharing," in Chapter 3) into a folder, or copy just the music files you want to use in MusicMatch Jukebox into a folder.

2. Copy the folder of music files to a disk that can be accessed (either directly or by a local area network) by the Windows-based PC.

3. Import the music files to your MusicMatch Jukebox library (as described in "Importing to MusicMatch Jukebox," in Chapter 1).

Switching from Windows to Mac

The iPod is specially configured with software for either a Mac or a Windows-based PC. If you purchased an iPod for Windows, you can reformat it to work on your Mac by using the iPod Software Updater, which lets you update or restore your iPod (available free from Apple Software Downloads at http://www.apple.com/swupdates/).

Switching from Windows to Mac reformats the iPod disk, wiping out all your music and data, and restores the iPod to its factory default settings, removing any custom settings. After reformatting, you have to update your iPod with music and information, and customize your settings again.

Note that once it is reformatted, your iPod will work only with Macs unless you reformat it again for Windows. You need Mac OS 9.2 or Mac OS X 10.1 or later to reformat an iPod for Windows into an iPod for Mac.

To update your iPod for Windows to work with the Mac, restoring the iPod to its default factory settings and reformatting the disk, follow these steps:

1. Connect your iPod to your Mac using the FireWire connection, as described in Chapter 1.

2. Open the iPod Software Updater application. If you downloaded the Updater, it is located in the Applications/Utilities folder. If you purchased an iPod with iPod Software 2.0, the updater is located on the CD-ROM that came with your iPod.

3. Click Restore. (In Mac OS X, you may need to click the padlock and type an Admin user's name and password first.)

4. An alert box appears to confirm you want to restore the iPod. Click Restore.

5. The iTunes Setup Assistant window appears, as described in Chapter 1. Continue with the setup by following the instructions that appear (refer to Chapter 1).

After following these steps, your iPod's hard disk has been formatted as a Mac HFS Plus disk.

You can transfer your MusicMatch Jukebox music library to iTunes, but only music in the standard MP3 and WAV formats are supported by both MusicMatch Jukebox and iTunes. Once your music is in the iTunes Library, you can update your iPod automatically, as described in Chapter 1.

To transfer your music library from MusicMatch Jukebox to iTunes, follow these steps:

1. Copy the music files linked to your MusicMatch Jukebox music library (as described in "MusicMatch Jukebox Music Libraries" in Chapter 3) into a folder.

2. Copy the folder of music files to a disk that can be accessed (either directly or by a local area network) by the Mac.

3. Import the music files into your iTunes Library (as described in "Importing to iTunes," in Chapter 1).

Adding Notes to Your iPod

You can add text notes, such as credits and liner notes about music, or information you need while traveling, that you can subsequently view on the iPod screen. To add notes to your iPod, follow these steps:

1. Create a text file with a text-editing or word-processing program (such as TextEdit on the Mac, or Notepad in Windows).

2. Save the text as an ordinary text file (with the filename extension ".txt").

3. Mount your iPod as a disk, as described earlier in this chapter.

4. Drag the text file to the Notes folder of the iPod, as shown in Figure 6.10.

Text files in the Notes folder are organized by filename. You can view these notes files on your iPod by choosing Extras>Notes and using the scroll pad to scroll the list of files alphabetically by filename.

Customizing Your iPod Settings

The Settings menu in the iPod's main menu offers ways to customize your iPod settings. You can change the main menu to have more choices, set the timer for the backlight, set the audible click for the button clicker, and more. Choose the Settings menu from the main menu. The Settings options include:

◆ **About:** Displays information about the iPod, including number of songs, how much space is used, how much space is available, the version of the software in use, the serial number, and the model number.

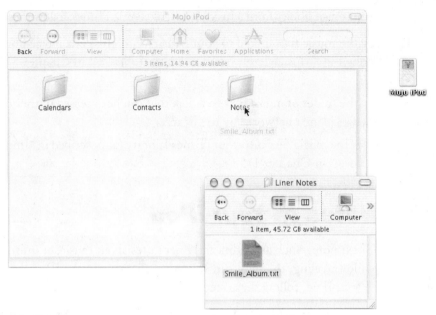

FIGURE 6.10 *Drag a text file to the Notes folder on the iPod.*

◆ **Main Menu:** Allows you to customize the main menu. For example, you can add items from other menus, such as "Songs" from the Browse menu, to the main menu. You can turn each menu item on (to appear in the main menu) or off.

◆ **Backlight Timer:** You can set the backlight to remain on for 2 seconds, 5 seconds, or longer by pressing a button or using the scroll pad. You can also set it to Always On.

◆ **Contrast:** You can set the contrast of the iPod display by using the scroll pad to increase or decrease the slider in the Contrast screen. If you accidentally set the contrast too dark, you can reset it by holding down the Menu button for at least four seconds.

◆ **Clicker:** When on, you hear a click when you press a button; when off, you don't hear a click.

◆ **Language:** Set the language used in all the menus.

◆ **Legal:** Display the legal message that accompanies Apple products.

◆ **Reset All Settings:** Reset all the settings in your iPod, returning the settings to the state they were in originally. However, your music and data files on your iPod are not disturbed.

To get the most functionality from your iPod, make sure you have the latest version of iPod software. To find out which version of software your iPod uses, select the About command from the iPod Settings menu. To update your iPod software to the latest version, go to www.apple.com/ipod and download the iPod Software Updater application.

Third-Party Utility Programs

The iPod has spawned a thriving industry of third-party accessories and products. Some of the most useful products are utility programs that expand the capabilities of the iPod or your ability to update the iPod, and even full-featured programs designed as replacements for iTunes and MusicMatch Jukebox. With so many programs to check out, you might be overwhelmed. I've selected three of the best programs (as of this writing) for the Macintosh and for Windows.

Keep in mind, with programs that allow music copying functions, that copying copyrighted songs to other computers without permission is illegal. *Don't steal music.*

Macintosh

On the Mac, third-party offerings have focused on extending the capabilities of the iPod and its software to do things like copying music from the iPod to the computer, and updating the iPod with contacts and calendar information.

iPod It 2.0.1

iPod It transfers personal information to your iPod from Entourage, Stickies, Mail, Address Book, and iCal. You can even download weather forecasts and news headlines directly to your iPod. iPod It is shareware available from www.ipod-it.com.

iPod Access v2.1

iPod Access lets you transfer songs from an iPod to a Mac. iPod Access is available from Findley Designs, Inc. (http://www.drewfindley.com/findleydesigns/).

iPodRip 1.5.1

iPodRip lets you transfer music from your iPod back to your iTunes Library, and listen to music directly on your iPod (saving disk space). It supports all iPod song formats, including MP3, AAC, Protected AAC, and Audible.com books. iPodRip is available from the little appfactory (http://www.thelittleappfactory.com/ipodrip.php).

Windows

On Windows, third-party offerings fill a void left by the lack of an Apple-branded iTunes-like program and the lack of an iSync-like program. There are lots more third-party programs for Windows, and they do everything from extending the capabilities of the iPod and updating contacts and calendar information to replacing the need for MusicMatch Jukebox itself.

iPodSync

iPodSync is a utility for Windows users to keep Microsoft Outlook calendars, contacts, tasks, and notes synchronized between a PC and an iPod. iPodSync exports to the iPod using the industry standard vCard format for contacts, and the iCalendar format for appointment information. iPodSync can even synchronize Outlook notes and tasks. For more information, see the iPodSync site (http://iccnet.50megs.com/iPodSync/).

EphPod 2.71

EphPod is a full-featured Windows application that you can use in place of MusicMatch Jukebox. It supports standard WinAmp (.M3U) playlists and can synchronize the iPod with a library of music files. It imports Microsoft Outlook contacts and lets you create and edit your own contacts. EphPod can also download the latest news, weather, e-books, and movie listings to an iPod. EphPod is shareware available from ephpod.com (http://www.ephpod.com/).

XPlay 1.1

XPlay provides both read and write access to your iPod hard drive for documents and data files, plus the ability to organize your music either from the Explorer-based XPlay interface or from Windows Media Player, as an alternative to MusicMatch Jukebox. XPlay makes your iPod appear as a normal drive under Windows for the sharing of data files, and makes your songs, playlists, artists, and albums appear in custom folders in Explorer, so they're easy to access and manipulate, and organized similarly to how the iPod organizes them. XPlay is available from Mediafour Corp. (http://www.mediafour.com/products/xplay/).

Chapter 7

Solving
Problems

Here's what you'll explore in this chapter:

◆ Troubleshooting when your iPod won't turn on or is not recognized by your computer

◆ Resetting your iPod

◆ Using the battery efficiently

◆ Updating your iPod's firmware and software

◆ Restoring your iPod to its factory default condition

This chapter describes some of the problems you might encounter with your iPod and computer, and how to fix them. If your iPod fails to turn on, or if your computer fails to recognize it, you will most likely find a solution here. You also learn how to make more efficient use of your iPod's battery power.

This chapter also covers updating the firmware and software on your iPod, and restoring your iPod to its factory default condition. That last option is a drastic measure that erases any music or information on the iPod, but it usually solves the problem if nothing else does. Finally, this chapter provides Windows-specific troubleshooting tips for solving problems unique to that version of the iPod.

Basic Troubleshooting

Problems can arise with electronics and software that can cause your iPod to not turn on, or not turn on properly with all its music and playlists. Problems can also arise in the connection between your iPod and your computer. The following are general problems that can occur and what you can do to fix them:

◆ If your iPod won't turn on, or it gets only as far as the Apple logo, or shows a folder icon (Mac only) with exclamation point, read this section for basic troubleshooting steps.

◆ If your computer does not recognize your iPod, see the sections "Updating Your iPod Firmware and Software" and "Restoring Your iPod" in this chapter.

◆ For specific problems involved with connecting iPod for Windows and using MusicMatch Jukebox, see "iPod for Windows Troubleshooting" in this chapter.

When you turn on your iPod, built-in diagnostic software checks the iPod disk for damage and attempts to repair it if necessary. If the iPod finds an issue when it is turned on, it automatically uses internal diagnostics to check for and repair any damage. You may see a disk scan icon on your iPod screen after turning it on, indicating that a problem was fixed. If this happens, you should update your iPod's firmware and software as described in "Updating Your iPod Firmware and Software" in this chapter.

The following sections describe basic troubleshooting steps to take if your iPod will not turn on, or if the Mac version shows a folder icon with an exclamation point on the Mac desktop (for Windows-specific troubleshooting, see "iPod for Windows Troubleshooting" in this chapter).

Checking the Hold Switch

If your iPod won't turn on, check the Hold switch position on top of the iPod. The Hold switch locks the iPod buttons so that you don't accidentally activate them. Slide the Hold switch away from the headphone connection, hiding the orange layer, to unlock the buttons. (If you see the orange layer underneath one end of the Hold switch, the switch is still in the locked position.)

Checking the Power

The battery may not be charged enough. If the battery is too low for normal operation, your iPod will not turn on. Instead, a low battery screen appears for about 3 seconds, then disappears. At that point, your only choice is to connect your iPod to an AC power source, wait for a moment, and then turn the power on by pushing any button on the iPod. If your source of AC power is your computer (using the FireWire connection), make sure the computer is on and is not set to go to sleep. The battery icon in the top-right corner of the display indicates whether it is full or recharging. For more information about maintaining a healthy battery, see "Maintaining Battery Life" in this chapter.

Resetting Your iPod

If your iPod is not responding and appears to be frozen, try resetting your iPod by following these steps:

1. Toggle the Hold switch: set the Hold switch to hold (lock), and then set it back to unlock.

2. Press the Menu and Play/Pause buttons simultaneously and hold for at least five seconds, or until the Apple logo appears.

3. Release the buttons when you see the Apple logo.

 WARNING

Releasing the Menu and Play/Pause buttons after the Apple logo appears is important. If you continue to hold down the buttons after the logo appears, the iPod displays the low battery icon and must be attached to power before it can work again.

After resetting, your iPod should work normally, with your music, data files, and most of your customized settings intact. If you want to also reset your customized settings, choose Settings>Reset All Settings>Reset from the iPod main menu.

Draining the iPod Battery

Battery-powered devices sometimes run into problems if the battery hasn't drained in a while. In rare cases the iPod might go dark and can't be reset until the battery is drained. If the above steps did not resolve the issue, disconnect your iPod from any power source and leave it disconnected for approximately 24 hours. After this period connect it to power and reset.

When Nothing Else Works

If you have tried the solutions above and your iPod will still not turn on, check the following:

◆ Make sure the iPod is the only device in your FireWire chain. While you can connect a FireWire device to another FireWire device that has a connection, forming a chain, it is not a good idea to do this with an iPod.

- Make sure you are using the FireWire cable that came with your iPod, and that the cable is in good condition.

- Try connecting your iPod to the built-in FireWire connection of a different computer to see if the symptom persists.

If you cannot turn on your iPod after performing these steps, it may need to be repaired. You can arrange for repair at the iPod Service Web site (http://depot.info.apple.com/ipod/).

If, after turning on your iPod, all you see on the display is the Apple logo and iPod name, and the device seems to be restarting over and over, try the following steps if you are using a FireWire connection to your Mac or PC (see "iPod for Windows Troubleshooting" in this chapter if you are using USB):

1. Connect your iPod to your computer's FireWire connection. (This procedure does not work with a USB connection, as it requires power.) Make sure the computer is on and is not set to go to sleep.

2. Reset your iPod as described in "Resetting Your iPod" earlier in this chapter.

3. When the Apple icon appears on the display, immediately press and hold the Previous and Next buttons until the""Do not disconnect" screen or FireWire icon appears. You can now restore the iPod—see "Restoring Your iPod" later in this chapter.

If the "Do not disconnect" screen or FireWire icon does not appear, repeat steps 2 and 3 (you may not have been quick enough in pressing and holding the Previous and Next buttons). If, after repeating these steps, the "Do not disconnect" screen or FireWire icon do not appear, your iPod may need to be repaired. See the iPod Service Web site (http://depot.info.apple.com/ipod/).

Maintaining Battery Life

To get the most out of one charge of the iPod battery, install the latest iPod software (see "Updating Your iPod Firmware and Software" in this chapter), use the Hold switch to keep buttons inactive until you need them, and put your iPod to sleep whenever you're not using it (see "Sleep Mode" in this chapter).

It also helps to keep the iPod at room temperature (generally near 20 °C, but you can use the iPod anywhere between 10 °C and 35 °C, or about 50 °F to 95 °F).

If you have left your iPod in the cold, let it warm up to room temperature before waking it from sleep. Otherwise, a low-battery icon may appear, and the iPod will not wake from sleep. If, after warming up, your iPod does not wake from sleep, connect the power adapter and reset your iPod as described in "Resetting Your iPod" in this chapter.

Sleep Mode

The iPod offers an automatic power-save feature (a sleep mode) as well as a sleep timer you can set.

The power-save feature automatically puts the iPod to sleep after 2 minutes of inactivity if you are not playing music.

If you are playing music, the iPod sleeps after the amount of time set for the sleep timer. The default setting for the sleep timer is off (never sleep). The sleep timer can be set from 5 minutes to 120 minutes, depending on the version of iPod software (see Chapter 6). If you set the timer to go off after a certain amount of time, the iPod sleeps after that time has lapsed. The sleep timer is then reset to off. You will need to reset it to an amount of time if you wish it to go to sleep again.

You can also put your iPod to sleep at any time by pressing and holding the Play/Pause button. If you turn off your iPod in this fashion while a song is playing, when it wakes the song will not play, and you will need to use the menus to select a song to play.

If your iPod sleeps while powered (either by FireWire or the Apple iPod Power Adapter), the charging status appears on the screen. When your iPod is not powered and sleeps, the screen is blank.

To wake your iPod, press any button. If you want your iPod to stay in sleep mode while it is in your pocket, you should deactivate all the buttons by sliding the Hold switch on the top of the iPod to the center.

Tips on Battery Use

Here are a few tips for using battery power efficiently:

◆ **Charging:** The iPod fast-charges the battery to 80 percent of capacity in an hour. However, it can take 3 hours to fully recharge the battery. Even in sleep, the iPod uses a small amount of current, and the battery slowly empties. Stored at optimal storage temperature, the battery will empty in 14 to 28 days.

◆ **Pause playing:** If you leave your iPod unattended, press Play/Pause to pause the song. If left playing, your iPod will continue to play songs until the battery is drained—particularly if the repeat setting is set to One or All.

◆ **Backlighting:** Backlighting can use a lot of battery power. If you don't need to use backlighting, turn it off. Choose Settings>Backlight Timer>Off.

◆ **Equalizer:** Turning off the Equalizer extends your battery life. To turn off the Equalizer, choose Settings>EQ>Off.

◆ **Avoid using Preview/Rewind or Next/Fast-Forward:** Avoid changing tracks by pressing the Previous/Rewind or Next/Fast-Forward buttons. The iPod uses a memory cache to open enough songs for you to listen to without constantly accessing the iPod's disk. This saves battery power. If you frequently change tracks by pressing the Previous or Next buttons, the cache has to turn on the disk to open the songs. This uses a lot of battery power.

◆ **Use compressed songs:** iPod's cache works best with songs of average file sizes (less than 9 MB). If your audio files are large, or uncompressed in the AIFF or WAV format, you may want to compress them, or use a different compression method, such as MP3, when importing them into iTunes or MusicMatch Jukebox (see Chapter 4). Also, consider breaking very long songs or tracks into shorter tracks that have smaller file sizes.

TIP

The iPod's battery icon in the top-right corner displays how much charge remains in your battery, but this status indicator is approximate. You may find that the battery indicator shows no charge left, but your iPod still plays, or you may see the opposite behavior—the battery shows a charge, but your iPod does not play. Either way, you should recharge the battery to a full charge, which takes about three hours.

Updating Your iPod Firmware and Software

You should be certain your iPod has the most recent iPod firmware update installed. To determine which version of the iPod software is installed on your iPod, press the Menu button until you see the iPod main menu, and choose Settings>About (in earlier versions, choose Settings>Info). You should see information next to "Version" that describes the software version installed on your iPod.

Macintosh Updating

For the Mac version, you can use the iPod Software Updater application to update or restore your iPod. You can download this application from Apple Software Downloads (http://www.apple.com/swupdates/). You can also determine the software version on your iPod by using iPod Software Updater: Connect your iPod to your computer, and launch iPod Software Updater. The iPod Software Updater window appears. The software version appears next to the "Software Version" heading. If this version of the iPod Software Updater application has a newer software version that it can install on your iPod, you will see "(needs update)" next to the version number. If not, you'll see "(up to date)."

The iPod Software Updater can update the software that controls the iPod and can also update the firmware for the iPod's disk, if necessary. Update does not affect the data stored on your iPod's disk.

To update the Mac version of the iPod's firmware and software, follow these steps:

1. Connect your iPod to your Mac. iTunes opens and, if set for automatic update, updates your iPod with its music library and playlists. The iTunes display notifies you when the iTunes music update is complete.

2. Quit iTunes.

3. Open the iPod Software Updater application (located in the Utilities folder, which is in your Applications folder). The Updater window appears.

4. Click Update. (In Mac OS X, you may need to click the padlock and type an administrator account name and password first. If the update button is grayed out, the software on your iPod is either the same version or a newer version than the iPod Software Updater application.)

5. When the program update is finished, the Update button is grayed-out, indicating that your iPod no longer needs an update. Quit the iPod Software Updater application.

Windows Updating

For the Windows version, you use the iPod Updater application to update or restore your iPod. This software was installed when you first set up your iPod for Windows using the iPod for Windows CD-ROM. The iPod Updater can update the software that controls iPod and can also update the firmware for the iPod's disk, if necessary. Update does not affect the data stored on your iPod's disk.

To update the Windows version of the iPod's firmware and software, follow these steps:

1. Connect your iPod to your computer. MusicMatch Jukebox opens, displaying the iPod in the PortablePlus window.

2. Quit MusicMatch Jukebox.

3. Open the Updater application by selecting Updater from the iPod menu in the Start menu (Start>Programs>iPod>Updater).

4. Click Update. (If the Update button is dimmed, the software on your iPod is either the same version or a newer version than the iPod Software Updater application.) A progress bar appears.

5. When the progress bar shows that the update is finished, the Update button is dimmed, indicating that your iPod no longer needs an update. Click the close box in the iPod Software Updater to quit the Updater application.

Restoring Your iPod

Restoring the iPod erases your iPod's disk and restores the device to its original factory condition. Restore erases all of the data on the disk, so make sure you back up any important data you may have put on your iPod. You can retrieve the music from your computer's music library.

Macintosh Restoring

For the Mac version, you can use the iPod Software Updater application to restore your iPod. You can download this application from Apple Software Downloads (http://www.apple.com/swupdates/). To restore the Mac version of the iPod, follow these steps:

1. Connect your iPod to your Mac. iTunes opens and, if set for automatic update, updates your iPod with its music library and playlists. The iTunes display notifies you when the iTunes music update is complete.

2. Quit iTunes.

3. Open the iPod Software Updater application (located in the Utilities folder, which is in your Applications folder). The Updater window appears.

4. Click Restore. (In Mac OS X, you may need to click the padlock and type an administrator account name and password first.) An alert box appears to confirm you want to restore your iPod.

5. Click Restore, and a progress bar appears. When the restore is finished, indicated by the progress bar, quit the iPod Software Updater application.

6. In the iTunes Setup Assistant window, type a name for your iPod in the space provided, and proceed with the setup as described in Chapter 1.

Windows Restoring

For the Windows version, you use the iPod Updater application to restore your iPod. This software was installed when you first set up your iPod for Windows using the iPod for Windows CD-ROM. To restore the Windows version of the iPod, follow these steps:

1. Connect your iPod to your computer. MusicMatch Jukebox opens, displaying the iPod in the PortablesPlus window.

2. Quit MusicMatch Jukebox.

3. Open the Updater application by selecting Updater from the iPod menu in the Start menu (Start>Programs>iPod>Updater).

4. Click Restore. A progress bar appears.

5. When the progress bar shows that the update is finished, the Update button is dimmed, indicating that your iPod no longer needs an update. Click the close box in the iPod Software Updater to quit the Updater application.

6. In the MusicMatch Jukebox Device Setup window, type a name for your iPod in the space provided. The "Complete library synchronization" and "Automatically Synchronize on Device Connection" options are selected by default, but you can turn them off if you prefer, as described in Chapter 1. Click OK to finish device setup.

7. Run MusicMatch Jukebox, select iPod in the PortablesPlus window, and click the Sync button to synchronize the iPod with the library of this computer. Wait until the synchornization is complete, as described in Chapter 1, and eject the iPod before disconnecting it from the computer, as described in Chapter 6.

iPod for Windows Troubleshooting

It's no secret that Windows is somewhat different than the Mac, and trouble-shooting a complex and varied Windows system can be a daunting task. You should install the latest updates and service packs from Microsoft to make sure your Windows system is up-to-date.

Follow these steps first if your Windows system does not recognize your iPod:

1. Check to make sure the cables are connected securely to your iPod and to your PC.

2. Wait until disk activity stops on your iPod. You can do this by watching the iPod's display. The disk activity indicator (two arrows spinning in a circle) appears in the upper-left corner of the display. Before ejecting or disconnecting, wait for the arrows to stop spinning.

3. Eject the iPod as described in Chapter 6. Then disconnect your iPod and reconnect it.

4. Quit MusicMatch Jukebox and reopen it.

5. Restart your PC.

If MusicMatch Jukebox still does not recognize your iPod, try restoring the iPod as described in "Restoring Your iPod" in this chapter.

As shipped from the factory, the iPod's disk is formatted as a Mac OS Extended format (HFS Plus) volume. When you install the iPod for a PC, iPod for Windows 2.0 software reformats the disk using the Windows (FAT32) format. If your iPod does not appear in MusicMatch Jukebox the first time you connect it after installing the software, the disk may be still formatted as a Mac disk. You can check the disk format in the About screen in the Settings menu. If it does not say "Windows," then reinstall the iPod software and check again to make sure it formatted the disk using the Windows (FAT32) format.

If your iPod does not appear in MusicMatch Jukebox, but "Do not disconnect" appears on the iPod display, open the iPod Manager utility and make sure MusicMatch Jukebox is the home application. The iPod Manager utility is provided with iPod for Windows to change iPod settings, launch the software updater, check the Apple site for updates, and change the home application for the iPod (set to MusicMatch Jukebox by default). To change the home application with iPod Manager, follow these steps:

1. Connect your iPod to the PC running Windows.

2. Click on the iPod Watcher in the system tray (or right-click the icon and choose iPod Manager from the pop-up menu), or open iPod Manager directly it by choosing Start Menu>Programs>iPod>iPod Manager.

3. Click "Change Home Application" and select MusicMatch from the drop-down menu.

4. Click OK to close the iPod Manager window.

5. Eject the iPod as described in Chapter 6, and then disconnect and reconnect your iPod.

If your iPod does not appear in MusicMatch Jukebox, but you see menus on your iPod's display, make sure disk mode is enabled in the iPod Manager utility, as described in Chapter 6.

If your iPod still does not appear in MusicMatch Jukebox, restart the Windows system while the iPod is connected. Occasionally the FireWire connection on a PC conflicts with another device or fails to work for some mysterious reason. You can tell when this happens: use the System control panel to view the Hardware panel, and click Device Manager. The Apple iPod IEEE 1394 device should be listed, and if it has a yellow exclamation point next to it, there is a conflict. You may be able to temporarily resolve the conflict by restarting Windows.

For more detailed information about Windows troubleshooting, visit Apple's support site for iPod for Windows (http://www.info.apple.com/usen/ipodwin/).

Chapter 8

Working
Magic

Here's what you'll explore in this chapter:

◆ Playing iPod songs with visual effects in iTunes or MusicMatch Jukebox

◆ Browsing online music with MusicMatch's Music Guide

◆ Accessing Web radio streams in iTunes and MusicMatch Jukebox

◆ Using smart playlists in iTunes to control automatic iPod updating

◆ Using the AutoDJ feature of MusicMatch Jukebox to create playlists automatically

◆ Cross-fading between iPod songs in iTunes, and using iTunes with iLife applications

◆ Using the iPod built-in diagnostic tests

This chapter describes tips and techniques for getting the most out of your iPod investment, such as playing iPod songs with visual effects in iTunes or MusicMatch Jukebox, browsing online music with the Music Guide in MusicMatch Jukebox, playing Web radio in iTunes or MusicMatch Jukebox, using smart playlists in iTunes to control the process of updating your iPod, and even using your iPod's built-in diagnostic tests.

Playing iPod Music through iTunes

Normally, when you connect your iPod to your Mac, iTunes starts up and automatically updates the iPod with your iTunes music library (unless you turned off the "automatic update" option in the Setup Assistant or changed it with the iPod button for iPod options, as described in Chapter 3).

To connect your iPod to play music through your Mac, see "Playing Music on Your Mac" in Chapter 2. During this process, you switch your iPod to update manually rather than automatically (by clicking the iPod Options button and turning on the "Manually manage songs and playlists" option. After setting the iPod to update manually, your iPod's name appears in full black and its song list appears when you select it. The iPod name can be opened like any other iTunes source in the list.

Playing Songs

You can play the songs on the iPod using iTunes so that the music plays through the Mac.

To play music on your iPod in iTunes, follow these steps:

1. Select the iPod name in the iTunes Source list.

    The list of songs on the iPod appears, and you can scroll or browse the iPod songs just like you would with the iTunes library (as described in Chapter 3).

2. Optional: View the iPod playlists.

    After selecting the iPod in the iTunes Source list, you can click the triangle next to its name to view the iPod's playlists.

3. Click a song in the iPod song list and click the iTunes Play button.

When you play an iPod song in iTunes, it's just like playing a song from the iTunes library or a track on a CD in iTunes—you have the same flexibility with playback. To play a song, click the song name, and then click the Play button. The Play button turns into a Pause button and the song plays.

When the song finishes, iTunes continues playing the songs in the list in sequence until you click the Pause button (which turns back into the Play button). You can skip to the next or previous song using the arrow keys on your keyboard, or by clicking the Forward or Back button next to the Play button.

The status display above the list of songs tells you the name of the artist and song (if known), and the elapsed time.

Rearranging, Repeating, and Skipping Songs

You can rearrange the order of CD tracks or the song list (or playlist) to automatically play them in any sequence, just like playing tracks in a programmed order on a CD player. Click the upward-pointing arrow at the top of the first column in the song list, and it changes to a downward-pointing arrow, with the tracks in reverse order.

To change the order of songs played in sequence, press and hold the mouse button on the track number in the first column for the song, and drag it up or down in the list.

To skip songs so they don't play in sequence, click the box next to the song name to remove the check mark. Unselected songs are skipped when you play the entire sequence. To turn off a series of check marks simultaneously, hold down the Command key while clicking a check mark.

You can repeat an entire song list by clicking the Repeat icon button at the bottom of the Source list on the left side of the iTunes window (or by choosing Controls>Repeat All). Click the Repeat button again to repeat the current song (or choose Controls>Repeat One). Click it once more to return to normal playback (or choose Controls>Repeat Off).

TIP

The Shuffle button (to the left of the Repeat button) plays the songs in the list in a random order, which can be fun. You can then press the arrow keys or the back and forward buttons to jump around in random order. Eject a CD by clicking the Eject button or by choosing Controls>Eject Disc.

Setting Up Visual Effects for the Music

When you play your iPod music through iTunes, you can display visual effects as with other music in your library or on CD. iTunes can display animated graphics synchronized to the music, using "morphing" techniques and patterns created by algorithm. Click the Visual Effects button on the bottom-right side of the iTunes window to turn on visual effects. The visual animation appears in the iTunes window and synchronizes with the music.

The Import button in the upper-right corner of the iTunes window changes into the Options button for visual effects. Click the Options button to open the Visualizer Options dialog box, as shown in Figure 8.1.

The Visualizer Options dialog box offers the following options that affect the animation, but not the performance, of iTunes playing music:

◆ **Display frame rate:** Displays the frame rate of the animation along with the animation.

◆ **Cap frame rate at 30 fps:** Keeps the frame rate at 30 fps or lower, which is the speed of normal video.

◆ **Always display song info:** Displays the song name, artist, and album for the song currently playing, along with the animation.

◆ **Faster but rougher display:** The animation plays faster, with rougher graphics. Choose this option if your animation plays too slowly.

FIGURE 8.1   *Setting options for visual effects in iTunes while playing iPod music through the Mac.*

The Visualizer menu in iTunes gives you even more control over visual effects. You can choose Visualize>Small or Visualize>Medium to display the visual effects in a rectangle inside the iTunes window, or Visualize>Large to fill the iTunes window. Choosing Visualize>Full Screen displays the visual effects full-screen. With full-screen visual effects on, you can click the mouse or press the Escape key on your keyboard to stop the display and return to iTunes. Choosing Visualize>Turn Visualizer On or clicking the Visual Effects button turns on the visual effects display.

While the animated visual effects play, press Shift+slash (/), as if typing a question mark, to see a list of keyboard functions. Depending on the visual effect, you may see more choices of keyboard functions by pressing Shift+slash again.

To turn off visual effects, click the Visual Effects button again. You can leave the effects on (except when in full-screen mode) even while opening the equalizer, because you still have access to the playback controls.

You can add more Visualizers for iTunes from freeware or shareware sites such as Version Tracker (www.versiontracker.com/macosx/).

Playing iPod Music through MusicMatch Jukebox

You can play the iPod's music directly on your PC using MusicMatch Jukebox. Normally, when you connect your iPod to your Windows-based PC, MusicMatch Jukebox starts up and displays the iPod in the PortablesPlus window. To play music from your iPod through your PC, follow the steps outlined in "Playing Music on Your PC" in Chapter 2.

When you play an iPod song in MusicMatch Jukebox, it's similar to playing a song in the library or a track on a CD—you have the same flexibility with playback.

Playing Songs in the Playlist

To play songs in MusicMatch Jukebox, you must first drag the selected songs from the iPod library in the PortablesPlus window to the MusicMatch Jukebox playlist window. The order of songs in the playlist is based on the order in which you selected them and dragged them to the list.

To play songs in the playlist, click the name of the song in the playlist window to start playing, and then click the Play button. When the song finishes, MusicMatch Jukebox continues playing the songs in the playlist in sequence until you click the Pause or Stop button. You can control song playback with MusicMatch Jukebox's Play, Stop, Pause, Next, and Previous buttons. The status display near the control buttons tells you the name of the artist and song (if known), and the elapsed time.

To rearrange songs in the playlist window, you can click on and drag a song from one slot in the list to another. You can use the Repeat button to repeat the songs in a playlist, and the Shuffle button to shuffle song playback in random order. For more information about creating playlists, see "Creating a Playlist in MusicMatch Jukebox" in Chapter 3.

Setting Up Visualizations for the Music

When you play your iPod music through MusicMatch Jukebox, you can display visualizations as with other music in your library or on CD. Visualizations are animated graphic images that change along with the music, using "morphing" techniques and patterns created by algorithm.

The animated graphics are displayed in the media panel to the right of the MusicMatch Jukebox player buttons (left of the playlist window), which usually shows the album cover art. You can click the Open button at the top of the media panel to display the Media Window, which shows the graphics in a larger window. You can create visualizations or choose a built-in visualization to display in this window. Visualizations play while your music is playing, and their algorithms maintain graphics that are synchronized to the music.

To choose a visualization, start a song playing and right-click inside the panel to show the context-sensitive menu, as shown in Figure 8.2. Choose Visualizations>Start/Stop from the context-sensitive menu. When the animated graphics start, right-click the media panel again to display the built-in visualizations available for use, as shown in Figure 8.3. Click the Open button at the top of the media panel to display the animation in a larger window.

FIGURE 8.2   *Right-clicking the media panel to choose visualizations in MusicMatch Jukebox.*

FIGURE 8.3   *Choosing a built-in visualization supplied with MusicMatch Jukebox.*

To create a custom visualization, follow these steps:

1. Start a song playing and right-click inside the media panel or Media window to show the context-sensitive menu, as shown in Figure 8.4.

2. Choose Visualizations>Select from the context-sensitive menu. The Select Visualization window appears, as shown in Figure 8.5.

3. In section 1 of the Select Visualization window, leave the first pop-up set to Visualization Editor, and set the Option pop-up menu to Visualization Editor.

4. Click the Configuration button to bring up the Visualization Editor, as shown in Figure 8.6.

FIGURE 8.4 *Choosing a custom visualization in MusicMatch Jukebox.*

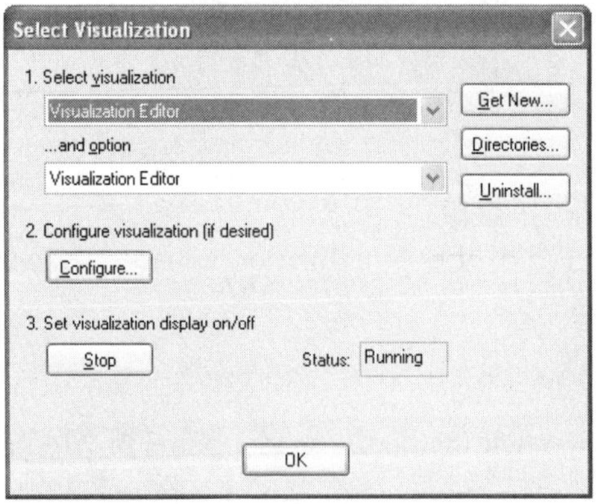

FIGURE 8.5 *The Select Visualization window for building a custom visualization in MusicMatch Jukebox.*

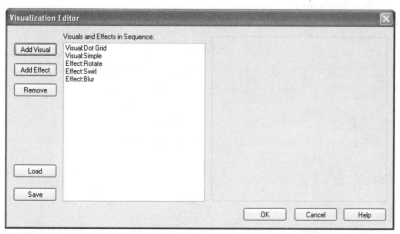

FIGURE 8.6   *The Visualization Editor lets you combine visuals and effects to create a custom visualization in MusicMatch Jukebox.*

5. Click the Add Visual button to add a color and pattern sequence. Click the type of visual you want from the drop-down menu. Once selected, the visual is added to the Visuals and Effects in Sequence box. Some visuals have settings that change the way they look. Highlight a visual in the Sequence box to view and adjust settings.

6. Click the Add Effect button to add morphing effects to the visual. As with visuals, some effects have settings you can adjust that control the behavior of the effect. Highlight an effect in the Sequence box to view and adjust settings.

7. Repeat Steps 5 and 6 as many times as you like, to combine visuals and effects.

8. Click OK to accept the changes in the Visualization Editor. Click OK in the Select Visualization window to start the animated graphics.

After creating a visualization you like, click the Save button to save your custom visualization. MusicMatch Jukebox provides a File Save dialog box pointed to the appropriate folder for saving custom visualizations, as shown in Figure 8.7. Use the Load button to load a saved visualization.

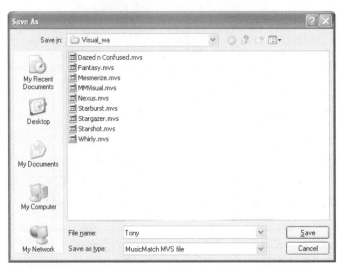

FIGURE 8.7 *Saving a custom visualization in MusicMatch Jukebox.*

Changing the Look and Feel of MusicMatch Jukebox

Like many Windows applications, MusicMatch Jukebox can change its look and feel by adopting "skins" that represent designs of the graphical user interface. You can also change your Windows wallpaper to show the album cover of the album you're listening to.

Using Skins

You choose a skin to give the program a certain look and feel, and the skin provides the same set of buttons to perform tasks such as increasing volume, opening the library, burning a music CD, and so on. Skins are changeable and cool to use when playing iPod music through your PC with MusicMatch Jukebox.

To change a skin:

1. Right-click inside the media panel to show the context-sensitive menu, as shown in Figure 8.8.

2. Choose a skin from the pop-up menu of skins that were downloaded or supplied with MusicMatch Jukebox.

3. After selecting the skin, MusicMatch Jukebox changes its look and feel automatically, as shown in Figure 8.9.

FIGURE 8.8   *Selecting a new "skin" (user interface) for MusicMatch Jukebox.*

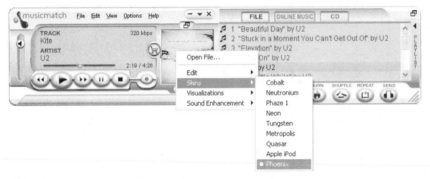

FIGURE 8.9   *Giving MusicMatch Jukebox a new look and feel.*

To download more skins from the Internet, first make sure you are connected to the Internet, and then follow these steps:

1. Choose Download Skins from the View menu in MusicMatch Jukebox. The Download Skins window appears, as shown in Figure 8.10, showing skins you can download.

2. Click on a skin in the Download Skins window. The skin downloads and installs itself automatically, displaying a progress window as shown in Figure 8.11.

After installing the new skin, you can switch from the newly downloaded skin to any other skin by right-clicking the media pane and choosing the skin from the Skins pop-up menu.

Learn how to make your own skins by downloading the MusicMatch Jukebox Skin Development Kit (SDK) from the Music Match Web site, www.musicmatch.com.

FIGURE 8.10 *Choosing new skins from the Download Skins window, which accesses the Internet directly.*

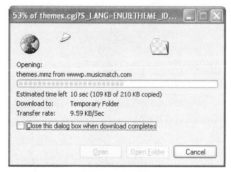

FIGURE 8.11 *Downloading a new skin with MusicMatch Jukebox.*

Changing Your Wallpaper

MusicMatch Jukebox can synchronize your Windows wallpaper to the CD cover art for each track you play (working with MP3, WAV, or Web radio streams). As you play each song, your Windows wallpaper changes to show the CD cover.

To set up synchronized wallpaper, choose Options>Settings>Display for the display settings, as shown in Figure 8.12, and in the Wallpaper section, turn on the "Use album art as wallpaper" option. Click the drop-down box and choose to display the cover art as tiles filling the screen (Tiles), or as an image centered on your Windows desktop (Center). Click OK to accept the changes to the Settings window. To turn off the wallpaper feature, turn off the "Use album art as wallpaper" option.

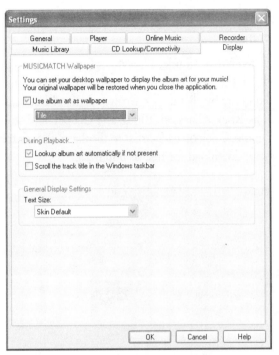

FIGURE 8.12   *Setting your Windows wallpaper as the cover art for the song playing in MusicMatch Jukebox.*

You must have already included the cover art in the song information tags. MusicMatch Jukebox looks up the cover art for you if you turn on the "Lookup album art automatically if not present" option (see Figure 8.12). When playing music in your library (or iPod music that is duplicated in your library), MusicMatch Jukebox looks up the cover art on the Internet and adds it to the song information (or "tags" the song) automatically. Purchased music is usually tagged with cover art already.

Using the MusicMatch Jukebox Music Guide

The MusicMatch Music Guide helps you find thousands of free MP3 files on the Internet and commercial music to purchase. You can search for and download free music, music videos, and photos from popular artists. Music Guide can also make recommendations based on your personal preferences, matched to other users on the Internet with similar preferences.

To open Music Guide, choose View>Music Guide. The Music Guide appears in place of your music library in MusicMatch Jukebox, as shown in Figure 8.13. You can find an artist or pick artists in a particular genre by clicking on Browse Artist. Here you'll find an extensive list of genres (such as Rock, Classical, Bluegrass, Gospel, and so on), or you can enter an artist or album name. Click on each artist to display a discography, the artist biography, and music you can download for free or purchase.

FIGURE 8.13 *Browsing music on the Internet with the MusicMatch Jukebox Music Guide.*

You can take advantage of the free music-matching service built into Music Guide, which finds music that suits your tastes based on your personal preferences. Music Guide compares your downloads and purchases to those of others who have down-loaded or purchased music, and provides recommendations based on matches.

To use the music-matching service, click the Recommendations button in the Music Guide window, and then click on the Sign Up Now button. Registration takes place automatically, and MusicMatch Jukebox compares your music with that of others who use the Music Guide. After a few minutes, the music-matching service has enough information and recommendations start to appear that match the music others with similar tastes have bought or downloaded.

While installing MusicMatch Jukebox, the default setting is to "opt in" to this ser-vice, which means it is automatically turned on. The service delivers recommendations based on personal preferences, but you may not want to share your information. If you choose to continue to participate in this feature, MusicMatch Jukebox periodically uploads your listening preferences so that the Music Guide can make better recommendations. However, if you don't want to participate, turn off the Personalize Music Recommendations option during installation.

To "opt out" of this service later, after installing the program, choose Options>Settings, and click on the General tab for the program's general settings. Turn off the "Upload user preference information based on listening profile" option. To "opt in" at any time, you can turn this option back on.

Turning On Web Radio

With iTunes on your Mac or MusicMatch Jukebox on your Windows PC, you can "turn on" and listen to broadcast streams from radio stations on the Internet that represent nearly every area of the world. You can tune into foreign and domestic music and talk radio, and even check out the local news and sports.

You can't record or save a song from a broadcast stream without special software (or by rerecording the stream as it comes into your computer). Therefore, it is not likely that you will put music from a Web radio stream into your iPod. But you can add your favorite stations to your music library or to a playlist to tune in quickly and easily. You can also tune in any Web radio or streaming broadcast if you know the Web address.

Web Radio in iTunes

iTunes offers built-in links to Web radio stations. To choose one, follow these steps in iTunes:

1. Click the Radio option in the Source list. The iTunes window displays a list of categories of radio stations, as shown in Figure 8.14.

2. Click the Refresh button to retrieve the latest radio stations, as more stations appear every day. The Refresh button in the top-right corner of the iTunes window (taking the place of the Browse button) connects iTunes to the Internet to retrieve the latest list of radio stations for each category.

3. Click the triangle next to a category name to open the list of radio streams in that category.

Radio station broadcasts are streamed to your computer—sections of the audio transfer and play while more sections are transferred so that you hear it as a continual stream. Some large radio stations offer more than one stream.

4. Select a stream and click the Play button, as shown in Figure 8.15. Within seconds you hear live radio off the Web.

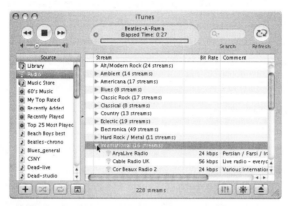

FIGURE 8.14 *Selecting a Web radio station in iTunes.*

FIGURE 8.15 *Clicking the Play button to play a Web radio stream in iTunes.*

If you use a modem connection to the Internet, you may want to choose a stream with a bit rate of less than 56 Kbps for best results. The Bit Rate column shows the bit rate for each stream.

iTunes creates a buffer for the audio stream so that you hear continuous playback with fewer Internet-related hiccups than most Web radio software. The buffer temporarily stores as much of the stream as possible, adding more of the stream to the end of the buffer as you play the audio in the buffer. If you hear stutters or gaps when playing a stream, set your buffer to a larger size by choosing iTunes>Preferences. In the Preferences window, click the Advanced button, and then choose a size from the pop-up menu for Streaming Buffer Size. Your choices are Small, Medium, or Large.

You can save the locations of Web radio streams in your music library in playlists. To quickly create a playlist from selected radio streams, first select the streams (by holding down Shift or the Command key to make multiple selections), and then choose File>New Playlist from Selection. To add Web radio streams manually to playlists, follow these steps:

1. Select a Web radio stream.

2. Create a playlist, or scroll the Source list to an existing playlist. (See Chapter 3 to learn how to create a playlist.)

3. Drag the stream name over the playlist name. iTunes places the stream name in the playlist with a broadcast icon next to it. You can click the playlist name and rearrange the playlist as you want, dragging stream names as you would drag song names.

Drag as many Web radio streams as you like to as many playlists as you like. Radio streams in your playlists play only if you are connected to the Internet.

Plenty of Web sites offer temporary streaming audio broadcasts for a period of time—a band might offer a broadcast from a tour for just a day or a week. All you need to know is the Web address, also known as the URL (Uniform Resource Locator). You can find most URLs from a Web site or e-mail about a broadcast. As of this writing, iTunes supports only MP3 broadcasts. You can find lots of MP3 broadcasts at www.shoutcast.com and www.Live365.com.

Once you have the URL, follow these steps in iTunes:

1. Choose Advanced>Open Stream. The Open Stream dialog box appears, with a URL text field for typing a Web address.

2. Type the exact, full URL of the stream, as shown in Figure 8.16. Include the http: prefix, as in "http://64.236.34.141:80/stream/1014."

iTunes automatically retrieves the streaming broadcast from the Internet and places it in your song list at the end, as shown in Figure 8.17. You can then play it or drag it to a playlist to save the location of the stream.

FIGURE 8.16 *Enter the URL to play any Web streaming broadcast.*

FIGURE 8.17 *Playing a Web streaming broadcast placed at the end of the song list in iTunes.*

Web Radio in MusicMatch Jukebox

MusicMatch Jukebox offers access to Web radio streams through MusicMatch MX radio with the following services:

◆ **MusicMatch MX:** Choose from 35 professionally programmed radio stations as well as exclusive stations and CD listening parties.

◆ **Artist On Demand** and **Artist Match:** Listen to a playlist of everything by a particular artist, and create custom radio stations based on up to 100 of your favorite artists.

◆ **Station Mixer:** Create one station that is a blend of several of your favorite MusicMatch stations.

◆ **Artist Sets:** Create playlists containing sets of tracks from particular artists you select, with your choice in the number of tracks for each set.

◆ **Era Radio:** Create stations based on one or more years and hear music from Billboard charts for the selected years.

◆ **My Station:** Hear a customized station based on the music you play through MusicMatch Jukebox, and MusicMatch MX.

To play Web radio, click on the Radio button (next to My Library) to display the MusicMatch MX opening window on the Internet, as shown in Figure 8.18. MusicMatch MX provides buttons for logging into your account (or setting up an account), and a navigation pane on the left.

FIGURE 8.18 *Using MusicMatch MX radio services.*

To play music from a Web radio station, click on the Radio Stations link in the left navigation pane, and stations will appear below the link. Click on a specific radio station, as shown in Figure 8.19, and click the "play this station" button.

You can adjust the sound quality with the Low, Medium, and CD buttons. You need to be an MX subscriber (by creating an account) to set Medium or CD quality.

It is possible to "capture" (essentially rerecord) a streaming broadcast using a third-party program such as the freeware package Audacity (http://sourceforge.net/projects/audacity/). By setting your Windows XP recording controls to use the "stereo mix" rather than the microphone for recording, you can redirect a stream to

FIGURE 8.19 *Selecting a radio stream in MusicMatch MX.*

Audacity, which you can use to create an MP3 music file. To redirect the stream, follow these steps:

1. Open the Sounds and Audio Devices in your Control Panel.

2. Click on the Volume tab, and then click the Advanced button.

3. Choose Options>Properties in the Master Volume window.

4. Click the Recording option for the "Adjust Volume for" section of the Properties window, and turn on the Stereo Mix option.

Super Tagging for Song Information in MusicMatch Jukebox

In MusicMatch Jukebox, you can enable the program's CD Lookup feature to grab song information from the Internet, as described in "The Internet and MusicMatch Jukebox" in Chapter 3,. However, if you are not connected to the Internet, or if you want to use different information, you can "tag" your music with information automatically using the super tagging feature.

Once your songs are recorded into the music library, select a group of songs or an entire album, and right-click the selection to display the context-sensitive menu (or choose Edit>Super Tag Playlist Track(s) with the album or songs already selected). Then choose one of the following:

◆ Choose Super Tagging>Lookup Tags to find and add information from the Internet. Even if you have partial song information, super-tagging can fill in the remaining tags. The Lookup Tags results window displays the tags found for each track. Choose the tag set that best represents your tracks.

◆ Choose Super Tagging>Tag From Filename to find and add information based on the music track's filename. For example, if the music file is named "U2-Beautiful Day.mp3" the tags created are "U2" for artist and "Beautiful Day" for the track title. In fields 1 through 4, as shown in Figure 8.20, you can set the parts of the filename to be used for artist, album, track title, and track number.

◆ Choose Super Tagging>Rename Files to change the filenames stored on disk to reflect a change in the artist's name (since music files are stored by artist name). MusicMatch Jukebox displays the current name and new name for each song, and you can click OK if you want to make the change. You can assign the parts of the filename to artist, album, track title, and track number. The Preview section shows the current filename and the new filename based on the four fields.

FIGURE 8.20 *Tagging (adding information to songs) based on the music track's filename in MusicMatch Jukebox.*

Repairing Broken Links in MusicMatch Jukebox

MusicMatch Jukebox can play songs located anywhere on your hard disk, but if changes occur to your hard disk's folder structure or to folder names, some of your songs may not be linked properly to MusicMatch Jukebox. Fortunately, you can repair these links automatically.

If you get the message "<path\track… could not be found…" while trying to play a track from your library, you can repair the link by right-clicking on the track and choosing Repair Broken Links (or by choosing Options>Music Library> Repair Broken Links). MusicMatch Jukebox scans your library for broken links and, as shown in Figure 8.21, offers the following buttons:

◆ **Fix It:** This button browses your hard disk for the file to re-link it to the library.

◆ **Remove:** This button removes the link from your library, but does not remove the music file from your computer.

◆ **Remove All:** This button removes all broken links. MusicMatch Jukebox searches your entire library and removes any links to tracks that are no longer active. However, it does not remove the music files from your computer.

◆ **Skip:** This button skips the current missing link and moves on to the next one.

◆ **Abort:** This button ends the repair process prematurely.

FIGURE 8.21 *Repairing broken links to songs in MusicMatch Jukebox.*

You should repair all broken links before synchronizing your iPod to your MusicMatch Jukebox library so that you don't miss any songs.

Smart Playlist Tricks in iTunes

Playlists are essentially lists of songs, as described in Chapter 3. "Smart" playlists can be created with iTunes that add songs to themselves based on prearranged criteria, as described in Chapter 3. The following are sample tricks you can perform with smart playlists in iTunes.

Limiting the Music for Automatic iPod Updating

If you have less space on your iPod than music in your iTunes library, your choices for updating are to update manually (by album, artist, or songs), update automatically by selected songs only, or update automatically by playlist. (You can't update the entire library automatically if it's too large to fit on the iPod.)

By combining the features of updating automatically by playlist, as described in Chapter 3 in "Updating by Playlist Automatically", and "smart" playlists, you can control the updating process while also limiting the amount of music you copy to your iPod automatically.

You can always update your iPod manually with the songs and albums you want (as described in Chapter 3 in "Updating Manually and Copying Directly"), but this method may be too slow. With the automatic update by playlist option, you can create playlists that you use exclusively to update your iPod. A "smart" playlist can be limited to, for example, 10 gigabytes (for a 10-GB iPod).

For example, in Figure 8.22, I created a smart playlist in iTunes that matches only songs in the "Rock" genre (specified with the Genre condition), limits itself to 10 gigabytes (specified in the Limit field and pop-up menu), and selects by highest rating.

FIGURE 8.22   *A smart playlist in iTunes that selects songs based on genre and ratings, but is limited to 10 GB for automatic iPod updating.*

This smart playlist, named "10g_list" in my Source list, can be used for automatically updating a 10-GB iPod. First, I change the iPod Preferences (after connecting my iPod—see "Updating by Playlist Automatically" in Chapter 3) to "Automatically update selected playlists only," as shown in Figure 8.23. Then I select "10g_list" as the only playlist to use when updating. As a result, when I connect the 10-GB iPod, iTunes automatically updates my iPod with the "10g_list" playlist, which is already limited to 10 gigabytes.

FIGURE 8.23 *Setting iTunes preferences for automatic iPod updating using the smart playlist.*

Using More than One Condition for Selecting Music

You may want to establish different conditions and selections in a smart playlist to refine your music selection to fit within your specified limit (in this example, the limit is 10 gigabytes for a 10-GB iPod, but you might want to use 20 or 30 gigabytes or some other limit). For example, you can refine your selection by adding more than one condition. To add another condition, click the + button at the end of the first condition to create a second condition, as shown in Figure 8.24.

When you add an additional condition, the "Match the following" option at the top (see Figure 8.22) changes to offer a pop-up menu with the choices "all" or "any."

◆ If you match "all" conditions, it is equivalent to using a logical "And" to combine conditions that must all be met before selection occurs.

◆ If you match "any" conditions, it is equivalent to using a logical "Or" to combine conditions in which only one must be met before selection occurs.

FIGURE 8.24   *A smart playlist in iTunes that uses two conditions for selecting songs and is also limited to 10 GB for automatic iPod updating.*

An example of using "any" is if you want to create a playlist with two or more artists. Add an additional Artist condition and set the "Match" option to "any" so that either artist is selected for the playlist.

AutoDJ Tricks in MusicMatch Jukebox

The AutoDJ feature of MusicMatch Jukebox provides a method of automatically creating and saving a playlist. (Playlists are essentially lists of songs, as described in Chapter 3.) To use AutoDJ, click the AutoDJ button on the Music Library window (or choose Options>Playlist>Auto DJ). The AutoDJ window appears, as shown in Figure 8.25.

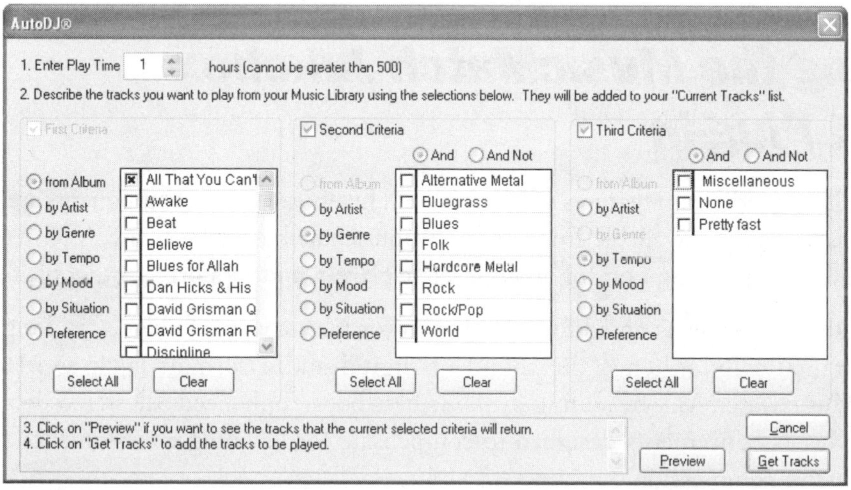

FIGURE 8.25   *Using AutoDJ to automatically create playlists in MusicMatch Jukebox.*

To create an automatic playlist with AutoDJ, follow these steps:

1. In the AutoDJ window, specify the playing time in section 1 by the number of hours. Entering 1 equals one hour; 0.5 equals half-an-hour (30 minutes), 1.5 equals one and a half hours (90 minutes), and so on.

2. In section 2, define what type of music to put into the playlist. In the left-hand column, decide the general type of music, or Criteria, used to create the playlist. Click any round button to the left (with round buttons, only one choice is possible). A list of available music options is displayed to the right.

3. Next, click on the check box to the right to activate any particular choices for the first criteria. For example, if you chose "from Album" as your criteria, you can click on the check boxes for multiple albums to select for the playlist.

4. If you turn on the Second Criteria, you also have a choice of specifying "And" to combine criteria so that both must be met, or "And Not" to use the second criteria to limit the results of the first criteria.

5. After making your selections, click the Preview button to see the songs to be added to the playlist and the actual playing time. By clicking the up and down arrows to the left of the Preview button, you can scroll through the specific songs selected.

6. To create the playlist, click the Get Tracks button.

Using the multiple criteria boxes, you can refine your AutoDJ selection as much as you wish to create a playlist that can be entertaining and also useful for timed shows.

Using the MusicMatch Jukebox DFX Plug-in

Plug-ins add extra features to MusicMatch Jukebox. Plug-in components are easy to install and are available from the www.musicmatch.com Web site, offering sound enhancements, support for other portable players, and support for other file formats.

DFX, available as an additional plug-in for MusicMatch Jukebox, is designed to dramatically enhance the sound of digital audio formats such as MP3 and MusicMatch MX by adding dynamic bass boost, enhanced 3D stereo depth, and other enhancements designed to compensate for listening environments and excessive compression.

To install DFX, you must be connected to the Internet. Choose View>Sound Enhancement>Select in MusicMatch Jukebox. From the Select DSP window, click on Get New, and a browser window opens that lets you select DFX. Click the link to download and install the plug-in, and MusicMatch Jukebox installs it automatically.

To use DFX, choose View>Sound Enhancement>Select in MusicMatch Jukebox. From the Select DSP window, click on DFX and click OK. Then choose View>Sound Enhancement>Show UI. The DFX interface opens in active mode.

You can drag the DFX sliders to the levels that fit your listening preferences, as follows:

- ◆ **Fidelity:** This setting controls the amount of high frequency harmonics that are regenerated and placed in the sound. With this control you can virtually eliminate the muffled sound of overly compressed music files.

- ◆ **Ambience:** This setting controls the amount of listening room ambience added to the sound, compensating for closely located speakers, poor listening environments, and sonic losses due to compression.

- ◆ **3D Surround:** This controls the amount of enhanced 3-D stereo depth added to the sound, compensating for monitoring limitations and sonic losses due to compression.

- ◆ **Dynamic Boost:** This controls the amount of additional loudness to be added to the sound. To get higher volume in the sound while also minimizing distortion, particularly with computer speakers, use this control to add additional loudness.

- ◆ **HyperBass:** This controls the amount of additional low frequencies to compensate for small speaker systems. It adds a deep, rich bass sound that greatly improves the bass performance of a portable sound system.

DFX also offers buttons for the following functions:

- ◆ **Presets:** Lets you select factory and user presets. Select the preset best suited for your music.

- ◆ **Save:** Lets you save the current effects settings as a preset, either as a new preset or as a modified version of the current preset. This button is disabled in the demo version.

- ◆ **Bypass:** Sends the input signal directly to the output, bypassing the DFX processing. When Bypass is active, the button is red.

To close DFX, choose View>Sound Enhancement and turn off the Show UI and Enable options.

Cross-Fading Playback with iTunes

You can fade the ending of one song into the beginning of the next one to slightly overlap songs, just like a radio DJ. iTunes is set to have a short cross-fade—a short amount of time between the end of the fade of the first song and the start of the fade of the second song. If you're playing songs on an iPod connected to your Mac, and songs from your iTunes library on your hard disk (or even a second iPod, both connected to your Mac), your songs will cross-fade automatically.

You can change this cross-fade setting by choosing iTunes>Preferences and then clicking the Effects button, as shown in Figure 8.26. You can turn the Crossfade Playback option on or off, and increase or decrease the amount of the cross-fade.

FIGURE 8.26 *Changing the amount of cross-fading (in seconds) between songs played using iTunes.*

Using iTunes Music in iLife Applications

While your iPod is supplied with iTunes, you may already have had iTunes because it comes with the iLife suite of applications for every Mac.

A day in the iLife might include ripping some music CDs with iTunes to use with your iPod on the road, and transferring the photos from your digital camera into your iPhoto library, then assembling a slideshow of the photos in iPhoto and setting it to music, which you have in your iTunes library. You can then bring video footage from your DV camcorder into iMovie and make a music video with all these elements. Finally, you can use iDVD to put together eye-popping menus and buttons to show off the music video and slideshow and anything else you may have, using the music in your iTunes library, and burn a DVD that your friends can play on an everyday DVD player.

Tunes for iPhoto Slideshows

Music makes a slideshow come alive, turning a set of interesting photos into something that resembles a documentary on television. iPhoto, part of the iLife suite of Mac applications, lets you organize digital photos into photo albums and slideshows, and you can set your slideshows to music from iTunes.

The Slideshow Settings window in iPhoto offers the option to play music. To use iTunes music with an iPhoto slideshow, follow these steps:

1. Open the Slideshow Settings window by selecting a photo album in Organize mode and clicking the Slideshow icon in the iPhoto tools pane.

2. Be sure the Music option is turned on in the Slideshow Settings window. A check should be in the check box next to the Music option, as shown in Figure 8.27.

3. Click the Music option's pop-up menu to select an iTunes playlist, or select iTunes itself to see the entire music library, as shown in Figure 8.27.

4. Select a song, and click the Play button to hear your selection.

FIGURE 8.27   *Viewing the entire iTunes music library in iPhoto to use music with a slideshow.*

Selecting by playlist is useful if you've already defined an iTunes music playlist for slideshows. The songs stored in the playlist you selected appear in the box below the menu, as shown in Figure 8.28.

FIGURE 8.28 *Viewing a playlist in the iTunes library in iPhoto to use music with a slideshow.*

If you selected the entire iTunes library in Step 3 above, the list of songs is initially sorted alphabetically by song title, but you can sort the list alphabetically by artist by clicking the Artist column heading, or sort the songs by duration (from shortest to longest) by clicking the Time column heading. Figure 8.29 shows an iTunes library playlist sorted alphabetically by artist.

You can choose only one song for a slideshow. iPhoto continues playing the song until it ends or the slideshow ends. If the slideshow repeats endlessly, the song also repeats when it ends. They play independently—the song and the slides are not synchronized. If you want to synchronize sound with photos or images, use iMovie.

Soundtracks for iMovie Movies

Music can establish a mood and make your movies a lot more exciting. You may want to synchronize actions in your video clips to musical moments or time videos

FIGURE 8.29   *Sorting the playlist songs in the iTunes library in iPhoto.*

to play at a certain rhythm with the beat supplied by a separate music track. iMovie helps you create music videos as well as videos with music, because you can edit videos to the music—using techniques such as slowing down and speeding up the video clips, using transitions, cropping and trimming clips, and so on. The music track can form the basis of the video.

iMovie gives you two tracks for adding extra sounds. However, you can overlay sounds in a single track, and iMovie automatically mixes all of the sound for playback, so the possibilities are endless.

To add music from your iTunes library to your movie, follow these steps:

1. Click the Clock icon in iMovie to switch to the timeline viewer.

2. Click the Audio button. The audio pane, shown in Figure 8.30, automatically opens your iTunes music library with a pop-up menu for selecting a playlist.

3. Select a song.

To select a song, you can do one of the following:

◆ Choose iTunes Library from the pop-up menu (if not already selected) and click a song (or scroll the song list if the song you want is not visible).

FIGURE 8.30 *Opening the iTunes library from within iMovie.*

◆ Choose a playlist from the pop-up menu, as shown in Figure 8.31, and click on a song in the playlist.

◆ Sort by artist first, and then scroll down to find the song you want, and click on it. The list of songs is initially sorted alphabetically by song, but you can sort the list by artist, as shown in Figure 8.32.

You can also use the Search feature by typing a word or even just part of a word, as shown in Figure 8.33, into the text field below the song list. (It has the word "Search" in the field, grayed-out, and you can type over the word.) The songs with those characters anywhere in the title show up immediately as you type.

After selecting a song, drag the song to the iMovie timeline viewer, or click the Place at Playhead button. The two lower tracks in the timeline viewer, as shown in Figure 8.34, are reserved for audio tracks. If you already moved the playback head to the exact spot where you want the music to begin, clicking the Place at Playhead button is easiest. The song becomes an audio clip in the audio track, which you can then adjust as needed to synchronize it with the video.

FIGURE 8.31   *Selecting a playlist from the iTunes library from within iMovie.*

FIGURE 8.32   *Sorting a playlist by artist in the iTunes library from within iMovie.*

FIGURE 8.33 *Searching for a tune in the iTunes library from within iMovie.*

FIGURE 8.34 *Using an iTunes song in the audio track of an iMovie sequence.*

Tunes for iDVD Slideshows and Menus

You can access your iTunes library from within iDVD to add a soundtrack to a slideshow to burn onto DVD, or to add music to your interactive DVD menus. iDVD is part of iLife and knows all about your iTunes library. You can go right to your iTunes library by clicking the Audio button at the top of the Customize drawer in iDVD, as shown in Figure 8.35.

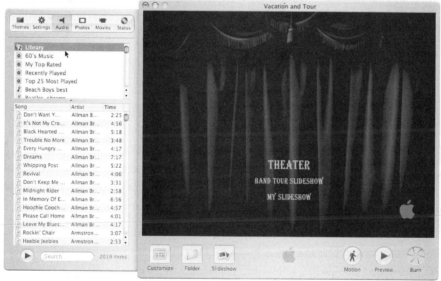

FIGURE 8.35 *Browsing the iTunes library in iDVD to add music to a DVD slideshow.*

To add music to a slideshow, follow these steps:

1. Click the slideshow text button for your iDVD slideshow to open the slideshow editing window. The slideshow text button is automatically created when you export the slideshow from iPhoto, or you can click the Slideshow icon to create a slideshow from scratch.

2. Click the Audio button in the iDVD Customize drawer. The iTunes library opens in the iMedia browser.

3. Drag a song from the iTunes library to the Audio icon in the slideshow editing window, as shown in Figure 8.36

The Audio icon in the iDVD slideshow editing window changes to show an icon for the type of sound file from iTunes—for example, an MP3 icon for an MP3 file or an AIFF icon for an AIFF sound file.

FIGURE 8.36 *Assigning a tune from the iTunes library to a slideshow in iDVD.*

The themes in iDVD used to design interactive DVD menus and buttons also lets you add music from your iTunes library to your menu background, which plays when the menu appears. To add a song from your iTunes library, follow these steps:

1. Select the theme in iDVD and click the Audio button to open the iTunes browser. The iTunes library opens, as shown in Figure 8.37.

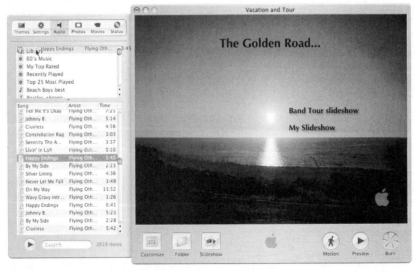

FIGURE 8.37 *Assigning a tune from the iTunes library to a menu background in iDVD.*

2. Select a song and drag it over the Settings button until the Settings pane appears, and then drop your song into the Audio well.

The song appears in the Audio well. The music plays in the background and repeats in a loop until the viewer clicks a button in the menu.

Running the iPod Built-in Diagnostics

Your iPod has a built-in diagnostics feature for testing the iPod's functions. To activate this diagnostic feature, reset the iPod as described in "Resetting the iPod" in Chapter 7, and when you see the Apple logo during the reset process, press and hold the Previous/Rewind, Next/Fast-Forward, and Select buttons simultaneously.

The iPod sounds a brief chirp, and in some models displays a backwards Apple logo. It then displays a list of diagnostic tests.

Summary of Diagnostic Tests

◆ You can select a test by pressing the Select button.

◆ Move forward to the next test by pressing Next/Fast-Forward, or move back to the previous test by pressing the Previous/Rewind button.

◆ To return to the list of diagnostic tests at the end of a test, press the Play button.

◆ To leave diagnostic mode, reset your iPod again, as described in Chapter 7.

The following diagnostic tests are offered:

A. 5 IN 1. This runs tests J through N below as a set of five tests.

B. RESET. You guessed it—this test performs a reset.

C. KEY. The button test. When you run this test, you have 5 seconds to press all the buttons of your iPod. As you press each button, the button name appears on the iPod screen. If you press all the buttons within 5 seconds, the words KEY PASS appears; otherwise the test fails.

D. AUDIO. This test checks the audio subsystem. If it passes, you see 0X00000000 DONE.

E. REMOTE. The iPod looks for the Remote Controller; if it fails to find it, you see RMT FAIL. If your Apple Remote Controller is connected to your iPod, the test should pass.

F. FIREWIRE. This test checks the iPod's FireWire connection. If it passes, you see FW PASS on the display. With earlier versions of the software, this test is **LIN REC** and can be used to record up to 6 seconds of sound through a line-in connection (which is not yet available as of this writing).

G. SLEEP. This test puts the iPod into sleep mode. To wake the iPod after this test, you need to perform a reset.

H. A2D. This test checks the power subsystem. If the power subsystem passes the test, you see 3.7V 0X000000E2 CHG OK FW 1 BAT 1 or four lines of similar code (depending on your iPod model).

I. OTPO CNT. This is a test of the scroll pad. As you scroll around the pad, the iPod displays a hexadecimal code representing the scrolling position.

J. LCM. This tests the iPod display. Press the Select button to go through each of three display patterns that test the display. With earlier versions of the software, this test is **RECORD** and can be used to record up to 6 seconds of sound through your earbud-style earphones.

K. RTC. This test displays a different hexadecimal code with each press of the Select button, which helps diagnose the effectiveness of the iPod's real-time clock. With some versions of the software, this test is called **CHG STUS**.

L. SDRAM. This test checks the iPod's RAM (random-access memory). If it passes, you see SDRAM PASS. With some versions of the software, this test is called **USB DISK**.

M. FLASH. This test returns the version of ROM (read-only memory) firmware in the iPod. With some versions of the software, this test is called **CHK SUM**.

N. OTPO. This test checks for scroll pad activity, and you must use the scroll pad instantly after activating the test, or the test fails. With some versions of the software, this test is called **DISPLAY**.

O. HDD SCAN. This test performs a scan of the iPod's hard disk and may take up to 20 miniutes to finish.

P. RUN IN. This test runs a series of internal diagnostic routines until you press and hold the Play button, which changes the display back to the list of tests.

Recording into Your iPod

I'm sure this heading got your attention. Your iPod is at the very early stages of its evolution as a consumer device, but even at this early stage, it has capabilities built into it that have not yet been exploited. Somewhere inside your iPod is the capability to record sound, but it has not been offered on the outside.

The proof is in the built-in diagnostics. In some versions of the software loaded onto the iPod, two diagnostic tests are provided that actually record and play back sound—test F (LIN REC) and test J (RECORD), as described in the previous section.

Test F is not that useful because there is no line-in connection you can use. But you can try test J to see how the iPod can record sound. Connect the Apple-supplied earbuds to the headphone connection, and follow these steps:

1. After resetting your iPod and activating the built-in diagnostics menu (as described in the previous section), use the Next/Fast-Forward button to navigate to J. RECORD, and press the Select button.

2. Speak into the left earbud of your earbud headphones when "BEGIN..." appears. You'll get about 6 seconds of record time, and then the iPod displays "DONE."

3. Press the Select button for playback.

4. When the iPod displays "PLAY END," press Play/Pause to return to list of tests.

The future for iPod is clear: someday this device will record as well as play. I hope to be around to use it for recording.

Appendix A

Shortcuts and Functions

MusicMatch Jukebox Keyboard Shortcuts

Function	Key Sequence
Play	Ctrl + P
Stop	Ctrl + S
Pause	Pause/Break
Jukebox Settings	Ctrl + Shift + S
Open Playlists	Ctrl + O
Make Playlist Active	Ctrl + F5
Open AutoDJ	Ctrl + D
Go to Previous Track	Alt + Left Arrow
Go to Next Track	Alt + Right Arrow
Increase Volume	Alt + Up Arrow
Decrease Volume	Alt + Down Arrow
Mute	Ctrl + M
Reduce to Mini View	Alt + Page Down
Open to Normal View	Alt + Page Up
Jukebox on top	Ctrl + T
Seek Backward	Alt + Shift + Left Arrow
Seek Forward	Alt + Shift + Right Arrow

iTunes Keyboard Shortcuts

Key	Function
Return	Play the selected song
Space bar	Stop the currently playing song
Command-right arrow	Play the next song in the list
Command-left arrow	Play the previous song in the list
Option-right arrow	Play the next album in a list
Option-left arrow	Play the previous album in a list
Command-up arrow	Increase the volume
Command-up arrow	Increase the volume
Command-down arrow	Decrease the volume
Command-Option-down arrow	Mute the volume
Command-E	Eject the CD
Option-Delete	Delete playlist and its songs from library
Shift-click the Add button	Create playlist from selection of songs
Command-click checkbox	Check or uncheck all the songs in a list
Command-I	Open song info window
Command-L	Show the currently playing song in the list
Command-]	Go to next page in Music Store
Command-[	Go to previous page in Music Store

iPod Function Summary

Shortcut	Function
Command-Option keys when connecting to Mac	Prevent iPod from automatically updating
Set Hold switch on and off, then press Menu and Play/Pause simultaneously for 5 seconds	Reset the iPod
Scroll clockwise while song is playing	Increase the volume
Scroll counterclockwise while song is playing	Decrease the volume
Press and hold Menu	Turn backlighting on
Press and hold Next/Fast-forward	Fast-forward through currently playing song
Press and hold Previous/Rewind	Rewind backwards through currently playing song
Press and hold Play/Pause	Turn iPod off
Press any button	Turn iPod on
Press Menu	Go back to previous menu

Appendix B

Web Sites for Information and Software

◆ **http://www.apple.com/ipod/**
Your first stop for iPod information and accessories is the Apple iPod site.

◆ **http://www.audible.com**
Get audio books and documents for the iPod from the Audible site.

◆ **http://www.apple.com/music/store/**
Visit the Web site for the Apple iTunes Music Store to learn all about online music purchasing.

◆ **http://depot.info.apple.com/ipod/**
Arrange for repair at the iPod Service Web site.

◆ **http://www.apple.com/swupdates/**
Download the iPod Software Updater application and current information about iPod software updates at Apple Software Downloads.

◆ **http://www.info.apple.com/usen/ipod/tshoot.html**
To solve problems with your iPod, visit Apple's troubleshooting guide on the Web.

◆ **http://www.ipodhacks.com/**
For comprehensive iPod information, tips, and tricks, as well as a lively user form, visit iPodHacks.

◆ **http://www.ipoding.com/**
For an excellent source of information about iPod accessories and third-party products, including downloads, visit iPoding.

◆ **http://www.ipodlounge.com/**
For lots of information about iPod third-party products, downloads, hacks, and tips, visit the iPod Lounge.

◆ **www.versiontracker.com/macosx/**
Download visual effects plug-ins (also known as Visualizers) for iTunes by visiting Version Tracker.

◆ **http://developer.apple.com/sdk**
You can download the iTunes Visual Plug-ins software developer kit (SDK) for free. (You must sign up for a free membership in the Apple Developer Connection.)

Index

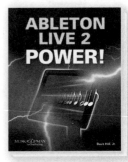